I AM who GOD says I AM

walking in the finished work of Christ

MUSA BAKO

DESTINY IMAGE™ EUROPE srl
Via Maiella, 1
66020 San Giovanni Teatino (Ch) —Italy

"Changing the world, one book at a time."

This book and all other Destiny Image™ Europe books are available at Christian bookstores and distributors worldwide.

To order products, or for any other correspondence:

DESTINY IMAGE™ EUROPE srl
Via Acquacorrente, 6
65123 - Pescara —Italy
Tel. +39 085 4716623 - Fax: +39 085 9431270
E-mail: info@eurodestinyimage.com
Or reach us on the Internet: www.eurodestinyimage.com

ISBN: 978-88-89127-94-0
For Worldwide Distribution, Printed in Italy
1 2 3 4 5 6 7 8 / 14 13 12 11 10

Dedication

I would like to dedicate this book to my Redeemer—the King of kings, the Lord of lords, Jesus the Son of God, the Firstborn from the dead, and the High Priest of good things to come—who loved me, called me, and anointed me despite myself to be doing what I am doing today. Your Majesty, You deserve the glory. To my family, the Redeemed Christian Church of God (RCCG), and Victory Assembly—I am proud to be part of you. Being your pastor inspires me—you are the best.

Acknowledgments

First and foremost, I would like to thank my God for helping me through this project. I would also like to thank my queen and my wife, Eunice Meque Bako. You are not only a beautiful woman on the outside, you are beautiful inside—you are kindhearted, resourceful, and an inspiration. Thanks for standing by me, thanks for being a perfect helpmeet, thanks for being patient, and thanks for your love. I owe everything to Jesus and to you.

I also want to thank my father in the Lord, Pastor E.A. Adeboye, the General Overseer of the RCCG who invested into me a lot of what I know today. Thanks for your excellent leadership, sir. I want to also thank God for the ministry of late professor Ishaya Audu, his fantastic wife Mummy Vicky Audu, and their investment into my life in the days of my little beginning. A big thank you to my mentor, Uncle Bayo Famonure, and his wife, my sister Naomi, who taught me to love missions and be poured out for God. You two are one of the reasons I am here today—thank you. I appreciate you, Pastor Agu Irukwu, for your inspiring leadership of the RCCG UK, and for your mentorship. Thank you for agreeing to write the Foreword for this book. You are the best at what you are doing. Thank you to Sarah Akpaka and Tamara Ng'ambi who helped to proofread my manuscript. Thank you to Vic and Diane Whittaker for helping with the second reading of this work.

I would also like to say a big thank you to Dorcas Rheece, Melissa Rangmen, and Jethro Men, my lovely children, for understanding when Dad had to be away on ministry. I love you.

Endorsements

I Am Who God Says I Am by Musa Bako provides an incredibly stable foundation upon which to build your life. There is such a huge amount of wisdom and practical advice rooted in Scripture that this book should be a textbook and not just a one-time read. It should be mandatory reading for every Christian who has within them a desire to succeed and reach their destiny. This book is a tool in the hand of every believer capable of lifting the reader out of defeat, poverty, and the mundane into a victorious, exciting journey which is destined in the end to be triumphant.

Ken Gott
Apostolic Team Leader
Bethshan Apostolic Community
Sunderland, UK

I Am Who God Says I Am is a practical handbook for the Christian life, providing every believer with the keys to rise above their situations and to walk in their God-given destinies. Pastor Musa Bako is an outstanding church planter, Bible teacher, and pastor, and he writes out of his wealth of experience from twenty years of ministry in such a way that will invigorate your heart and soul. This is a book that will rekindle lost hopes and dreams, not only inspiring you to dream of achieving greatness, but also giving you tools to get there and helping you to deal with all the limitations before you. Regardless of who you are or where you have been as a Christian, this is a must-read book, and I unreservedly recommend it to you!

Reverend Mike Breen
Former Rector, St. Thomas' Church Sheffield, UK
Author, Global Team Leader of 3 Dimension Ministries
Senior Guardian of the Order of Mission
South Carolina, USA

Pastor Bako has a heart and passion for the people of God. He has been used of God to help many on their path to destiny in God. Having known him for many years, I can say he is indeed one of God's fire brands for these end times. It is out of this passion he has written this book to help more people in God's vineyard. You will be blessed as you read this book and interact with God's grace in the life of the author. May you be all that God wants you to be, and may this book be one of the tools that will propel you along this life's journey.

Reverend Kola Ewuosho
Fountain of Wisdom Ministries, UK

Pastor Musa Bako has spent much time writing and recording his thoughts on how the Kingdom of God operates and flows. Within this book are keys to honoring God, walking in faith, and seeing God pour out His blessings to you and your church. Within it are nuggets for the soul and much food for thought. As a fellow pastor in Sheffield, I wish him all the best with its publication.

Dave Gilpin
Senior Pastor, Hope City Church
Sheffield, UK

Contents

Foreword

A rguably the greatest challenge that faces us today is one of identity. As that wise king so eloquently put it, *"As he thinketh in his heart, so is he..."* (Prov. 23:7). For too long, the saints of God have been robbed of their identity by their adversary as a result of the lies and deceptions that have been placed in their minds. This has also been reinforced by challenges of trials and afflictions, leaving man with a wrong picture of himself imprinted on his mind. The result of this is that so many in the Kingdom of God are living below the standard God intends for them.

The solution is actually quite straightforward. This flawed picture needs to be erased and replaced with the right one. Paul puts it so aptly:

> *And be not conformed to this world: but be ye transformed by the renewing of your mind, that ye may prove what is that good, and acceptable, and perfect, will of God* (Romans 12:2).

What is needed is to delete wrong information and replace it with right information. In doing this, we destroy patterns that restrict or hinder openness and replace them with patterns that promise the prosperity of our soul and spirit. This is precisely what this book does.

It starts by establishing what is so foundational—the encounter with God and the integrity of God—and takes the reader on a journey that leads them to achieving their destiny. With the Bible as a clear reference point, Musa Bako uses very simple language to convey deep, simple truths. You cannot fail to be filled with optimism, hope, and faith as you read this book. Enjoy!

Pastor Agu Irukwu
Senior Pastor, Jesus House for All Nations
London, UK Chairman for Executive Council
Redeemed Christian Church of God, UK

Introduction

Many people are born into existence and depart, however, only a few people make a meaningful impact in their lifetimes. Only a few people discover their purpose, turn it into passion, and fight for it like they do not have any other option. These are the people who, as a result of their pursuit, attain to greatness. This book was inspired as a tool to show you that you can achieve greatness in life and there is no limitation before you, because you are born, blessed, and ordained to be great. It does not matter what anybody is saying concerning you, and it does not matter what you have been through in life. All these cannot change how God sees you; neither can anything alter what He has planned for you.

God destroyed the power of satan over you the day you came into a relationship with Jesus. He stripped him of every power over your destiny. He broke every curse over you the day you gave your life to Jesus and became born again. You see, by virtue of your conversion you are not only empowered, you are placed on that path that leads to accomplishing the purpose for which you were created. The road map to your destiny is the Word; you are everything God has said you are in His Word. God means whatever He says. You are who He says you are, but you have to know what His Word says about you; you have got to believe it and act like it is so. When you know what the Word of

God says and you believe it and you act on that Word as if it is so, it nurtures your spirit and it prospers your soul (see 3 John 1:2).

The prosperity of the soul is significant in the interpretation of the ministration of the Spirit of God, but we often do not talk about the prosperity of the soul. Actually, our physical prosperity is dependent on how we prosper in our soul. What happens in your soul determines your well-being. The soul consists of the mind, the will, and the emotions. Your mind, will, and emotions to a large extent determine your behavior and what you are going to become in life, because they contain your knowledge and your desires and they determine the choices you make which, in turn, forms your behavior. Your behavior ultimately determines what you are going to attract to you.

If you are not prospering in the soul, you will walk in ignorance of God's will for you, you will have low self-esteem and a bad image of yourself, and you will not reach your highest potentials. To prosper in your soul, you will need to commit to feeding on the Word. You need to feed on the Word just as you need food to nourish your body. You need the Word to be healthy in your spirit and in your soul (see Matt. 4:4). Just as you need to eat a healthy, balanced diet when feeding your physical bodies, be balanced when feeding your soul. Do not only dwell on what God is saying about something you have an interest in—feed on everything. Learn everything that there is to learn in the Bible.

If all you are feeding on is one aspect of life, you will prosper only in that aspect and suffer want in other aspects. For instance, you can enjoy divine health and not be financially blessed. You cannot be financially blessed if you think that it is a sin to have large amounts of money, live in a bigger and better house, and drive a new car even if you are walking in holiness. You cannot be successful in life or financially blessed if you think that it is not for people like you or if you think that you can never become outstanding and have plenty financially. You cannot be healed if you think that the sickness you have is a family thing and nothing can be done about it. You cannot be healed if you think that your sickness is OK because it makes you humble.

What you believe will determine what you get in life. What you believe is determined by what you know. You are enlightened only in the direction your soul is fed. Life responds to what you know. What you feed your soul will determine your thinking, your beliefs, your choices, and your behavior. Your behavior will determine what you attract, and what you attract will determine how great you can become in life.

Fear is the product of the soul. If it builds a stronghold in your soul, it stands in the way of your prosperity. Fear has power like faith does. However, whereas faith attracts positive forces, fear attracts negative forces. Just as what you have faith in comes to pass, what you fear will come to pass too. When your soul is prospering, fear vanishes and you develop power, love, and a sound mind (see 2 Tim. 1:7).

Power is about having the boldness to face the challenges of life. We need to be bold because life is full of battles. Power is also about being bold to follow God's leading even when it appears to be unpopular or not comfortable. Power is about being bold to take a stand even when it means standing alone.

Love is the ability to relate to people and not harm them. It is the power to do good to people who have shown themselves to be friends as well as those who have treated us as enemies (see Rom. 12:21).

Soundness of mind is the ability to prove the good and perfect and acceptable will of God (see Rom. 12:2). When your soul prospers in the Word, you are able to discern the perfect and acceptable will of God; you are able to see the world in a new light and are able to interpret your situation, not as other people see it, but in the light of the Word. When you have a sound mind, you will be making good judgments, you will be having inspired and godly ideas, and you will be creative in your thinking. Having a sound mind is seeing yourself as God sees you (see 1 Cor. 2:9-12).

Resourcing men and women
to succeed in life
and fulfill the reason for
which they were created.

Chapter One

Encounter With God

And ye shall seek Me, and find Me, when ye shall search for Me with all your heart. And I will be found of you, saith the Lord: and I will turn away your captivity, and I will gather you from all the nations, and from all the places whither I have driven you, saith the Lord; and I will bring you again into the place whence I caused you to be carried away captive (Jeremiah 29:13-14).

God desires to reveal Himself to you personally and in a practical way. He wants you to know Him; He wants to demonstrate His greatness, His wonder, His majesty, His goodness, and His power in you and through you. He called you so you can be the witness of God to humanity. The world can know and see God through you, and that can happen when you encounter Him. When a person truly encounters God, he becomes aware of His presence like never before. The fear of God will come upon him and rise inside him, and there will be genuine conversion. When a person encounters God, he will start to live a selfless life, devoted to God, and he will become bolder and able to believe God for anything, even when it seems physically impossible. It is in an encounter with God that we know Him deeper, encounter the supernatural, and experience transformation. The essence for this chapter is to encourage you to desire to encounter God and know Him in a deeper way, more personally than you ever have.

PERSONAL ENCOUNTER

When someone encounters God personally, he is never the same again. He will start to understand and experience the goodness and mercies of God like never before. His fears will vanish, sickness can't have power over his body, and the fear of death loses its grips on him. He will walk in favor and will succeed where other people are failing.

We can have an experience of God in many ways. We can experience Him through a miracle, through healing, or through an atmosphere of worship, and this is where a lot of believers are. They know so little of God and their faith is hanging on their pastor and their prophets. God wants us to know Him personally and walk with Him, not only experience His acts.

We encounter God through our spirit, so the believer must learn to walk in the spirit. It is in this kind of walk that he can encounter God. The born-again believer's spirit is regenerated and brought into a level where he can know God, hear God, and experience Him. We need to desire to have a personal encounter with God. If you look at Moses you will see that experiencing the acts of God did not satisfy him. The burning bush did not satisfy him. The demonstration of God's might through the plagues in Egypt and bringing Israel out of captivity did not satisfy Moses. He wanted more of God, he wanted to see God face to face, and he asked God for it. When God showed His glory to Moses and proclaimed the goodness of God, something about him changed. When we truly encounter God, believe me, something about us will change. One encounter changes lives; one encounter can take you to a higher level with God.

A lot of us have experienced the wonders of God, miracles, breakthroughs, and some blessings of God. In worship we have experienced the warmth of God, but there is more to experience. My desire is that you will encounter Him, walk with Him, and know Him deeper and deeper. If you are born again, you are brought to that place where you can experience and know God. Through the born-again experience, your spirit was regenerated, quickened, and united with God. Through your regenerated spirit you connect with God. Flesh and blood cannot encounter God. We experience God through our spirit; the spirit is the connecting link between God and man.

> *But there is a spirit in man: and the inspiration of the Almighty giveth them understanding* (Job 32:8).

God's original purpose is for man to be led by his spirit, not the soul nor the body. Without the function of the spirit, everything is dead. When a believer is not walking in the Spirit—when his spirit is not empowered, when he is not guided by the Spirit or motivated by the Spirit—everything is dead. The material man must be subject to the spirit man. When the spirit in man connects with God, it receives illumination and understanding. When your spirit is weak and not in tune with God, you do not connect with God. The spirit is what connects you with the Divine, because that is the divine part of you.

When you are not in tune with God, you walk in the flesh. The flesh operates in two realms—the realm of the soul and the body. The soul ministers through the voice of reason, and the body ministers through the voice of feeling. You cannot know nor walk with God by the spirit of man, following the voice of reason or feeling. We are going to be looking at this in more detail later on when we will be looking at knowing and following the leading of the Holy Spirit.

The spirit ministers supernaturally because it is able to connect and take from the realm of the divine and show it to man. The way of the spirit may go against the voice of reason and feeling. The body may not feel like it, the senses may not feel like it, but it does not matter, because in the spirit you are walking in the divine, the supernatural, and the extraordinary. When you walk that way, you will start to show forth your sonship, manifesting the power of God. God is seeking to demonstrate His power through you. Even the creatures can't wait for your manifestation. When you are walking in the Spirit, you are able to bring the flesh and all its desires to subjection and you are able to walk with God (see Rom. 8:10; Gal. 5:16).

The believer needs to pay more attention to his spirit and seek to nurture and develop it more than he does the other parts. When you don't develop your spirit, you understand little of spiritual things and you can hardly hear God or understand Him when He speaks. It is little wonder how few believers today really understand the voice of God. They are basically followers of men and can easily fall prey to lying spirits. You hear a lot of, "My pastor said," among believers; that is all they are holding on to and walking with. So what happens when the pastor gets it wrong and is misinterpreting the Bible? They can get it wrong, too. I understand that pastors are put in the church to feed the Body, and church folks should trust them to get it right, believe in what they teach, and submit to their authority. I am a pastor, too, and I like my church folks to treat me that way, but we must understand that the pastor's primary mandate is to help the believer to grow, mature in the things of God, understand God for himself, and be able to receive from Him for himself. Every believer owes it to himself to cultivate and develop his spirit.

We must develop the spirit man to connect with the Divine, and to develop our spirit we will need to feed it. When we do not feed the spirit, it becomes lean and weak. When the spirit is lean, an interruption occurs in its flow with God. In this state, the flesh gains more control and begins to lead man, instead of the spirit as God intended. When the believer is in the flesh, he cannot connect with God, because God is a Spirit. He is not able to walk by faith or in the supernatural, because the flesh does not understand the way of faith. The spirit is strengthened when it dwells in the place of prayer, when it feeds on the Word, when it celebrates in praise and worship, and when it is in constant fellowship with the brethren.

The prayer that feeds the spirit is the one that communes with God and not the "Bless me, deliver me, help me" type of prayer. You need to have a deep desire for God that pushes you into the place of prayer, not only a desire to pray because some things are not right in your life and you need God to fix them for you. Also, it is not the quick ten- or fifteen-minute prayer that develops the spirit. The minimum time will be an hour, as we saw in the experience of Jesus in the Garden of Gethsemane when He challenged His disciples about tarrying for an hour with Him (see Matt. 26:40). The believer needs to learn to wait in the presence of God in the place of prayer (see Isa. 40:31). It is the deep desire for God that can keep you in the presence of God; without it, it will be a hard work. The psalmist says:

> *One thing have I desired of the Lord, that will I seek after;*
> *that I may dwell in the house of the Lord all the days of my life,*
> *to behold the beauty of the Lord, and to enquire in His temple*
> (Psalm 27:4).

The study of the Word that feeds the spirit is not reading the Bible to memorize it. It is good to memorize Scripture, as it also helps to renew your mind. That way, you store the Word in your mental faculty and are able to retrieve it when needed. However, to feed the spirit man, you will also need to learn to meditate on the Word. Meditation is the process through which you deliver the Word into your spirit. And you know that your spirit is fed only when the light of the Word starts to shine in you, when you've broken through the letters and have received the *rhema* word, or revelation knowledge. It is when God breathes the Word in your spirit and it becomes alive in you.

Every word that you have received will sometimes get attacked. Situations will arise to attack your knowledge of the Word, and if all you have done is feed the mind through memorization, you are going to start to doubt and walk in unbelief. But if you have fed your spirit through meditation in the Word and have received revelation knowledge, you are going to hang in there no matter what. When the Word is in your spirit, the devil can't steal it.

You can encounter God personally, and He wants you to. When you do, it will revolutionize your entire life. Your relationship with God will gain a new dimension, your faith will rise, and the way you look at life will change. For that to happen, you must start to desire Him more than the things of this life. Spend time in His presence— much time—develop your spirit, and cultivate it so it can become more sensitive and aware of the presence of God.

HOPE AGAINST HOPE

Why art thou cast down, O my soul? and why art thou disqui-
eted in me? hope thou in God: for I shall yet praise Him for the
help of His countenance (Psalm 42:5).

The Lord has been encouraging me lately to renew my hopes and
expectations and not to allow them to die, no matter the challenges
or the odds. I think this is because there are quite a number of things
which I have hoped for and thought I would have achieved by now, but
I have not yet achieved them. The Bible says, "Hope deferred maketh
the heart sick: but when the desire cometh, it is a tree of life" (Prov.
13:12). When what you are hoping for seems very distant, and when
there is no physical evidence that you are making progress on your
way there, you feel like you are only chasing shadows—like you are
on the road to nowhere.

I do not know if you are currently at this point in your life and
feeling low and hopeless. As I have been encouraged by the Lord, I
would like to encourage the reader whose hope is waning to keep it
alive and not let it die. Against all hope, keep hoping. He that has
promised will fulfill what He has said concerning you. That was what
Abraham did, and God imputed righteousness unto him. The Bible
says that against hope, he hoped in God.

Who against hope believed in hope, that he might become the
father of many nations, according to that which was spoken,
So shall thy seed be (Romans 4:18).

To "hope against hope" means to be confident that something that
you expect to happen will happen, even though there is no physical
evidence to show that it will happen. Hope is knowing that there is
something out there for you, and you are expecting it to happen.

Hope is different from faith. Faith is holding firmly onto hope.
Faith is the confidence that that which is hoped for will happen.
Faith is the power that sustains hope when what is hoped for seems
physically unlikely. Hope is the expectation for something in the
future. It is possible to hope and not have faith, but it is not possible to

have faith without hoping for anything, because faith is the substance of things hoped for. Faith cannot exist without hope. Hope requires faith to be alive, but faith requires hope to exist. For without hope, there cannot be faith.

KEEPING HOPE ALIVE

It is only when your hope is kept alive—even when things seem to be going against you—that it can be said that you have faith. Yes, it can be hard to be hopeful when bad things are happening in our lives and when we cannot see any light at the end of the tunnel. But my challenge to everyone reading this book is to not let your hope die, but to keep expecting and waiting for something better, no matter the odds against you. You have got to hope against hope. Keep it alive! You are who God has said you are, and you shall be manifested.

Some people think that it is better not to be too hopeful about anything in life. They say that it is better to not hope for anything in life, since there is no guarantee that what you are hoping for will come to pass and in order for you not to get hurt or disappointed in case something does not happen. They say, "Whatever will be, will be." But, you see, it costs more to live in hopelessness than in hope.

Hopelessness will steal your self-worth, steal your confidence, cause you not to dream, and make you feel like a loser. Hopelessness will make your life a sad life. Think about living without expectations in life. Think about living and not knowing your future will be bright. Think about getting into a relationship and not knowing what will become of it. Think about starting a course and thinking you might not finish well. Think about starting a business and expecting it to collapse. Think about setting out on a journey and not knowing whether you will get there. A life without hope is a life of misery. Without hope, you do not have a future. Hope paints a picture of tomorrow. Hope makes you a fighter. Hope makes you look out for answers and solutions. It keeps you going. Hope keeps your spirit energetic. The joy of being alive is our hope for the future.

The devil may attack anything in your life. He may touch your career, your studies, your health, your relationships, and your finances. You may even stumble and fall in your walk with God. Things might go wrong everywhere you turn. Whatever satan does, do not let him kill your hope; do not let him take away your confidence. Do not let him quench your enthusiasm about the future. You cannot afford to become despondent or have a carefree attitude about life. Don't be somebody who says, "I will just do the best that I can and leave the rest to God. I don't really expect anything. Whatever will be, will be." God wants us have desires. He wants us to be people of hope, believing Him for a great future. He wants us to have expectations so He can fulfill them.

> *It is good that a man should both hope and quietly wait for the salvation of the Lord* (Lamentations 3:26).

You need to have expectations in life. Until you hope for a thing, it may not happen for you. A hopeless life is a purposeless life, a life lived in waste. No matter what, do not let your hope die. I challenge you to keep it burning. You are who God says you are, even if you do not see it happening.

DO NOT DWELL ON THE PAST

> *Brethren, I count not myself to have apprehended: but this one thing I do, forgetting those things which are behind, and reaching forth unto those things which are before* (Philippians 3:13).

You have got to learn not to dwell on your past—not on your past failures, setbacks, or disappointments. There are many disappointments in life—and believe me, they happen to everybody—but it is how we deal with them that counts. That you have experienced all the bad things of life does not mean that it is the end for you. It is not the end for you until you allow the past and present challenges to cloud the future. When you start to concentrate on the number of times you have tried and failed and all the hardship you have been through and how nobody really cared, then you will make room for self-pity to set in. You will allow low self-esteem and discouragement to take over, and that will kill the fighting spirit in you.

The past is past; what counts now is where you want to go from here and what you need to do to get there. Failure in the past is not the end of your life. There is a story behind every great person, and there is a story behind every success. A good example for us is the story of Abraham Lincoln, the sixteenth president of the United States of America.

ABRAHAM LINCOLN

- 1816: His family was forced out of their home and he had to work to support his family.

- 1818: His mother died.

- 1831: The business he started failed and he lost everything.

- 1832: He stood for election in the legislature and was defeated.

- 1832: He lost his job and could not get into law school.

- 1833: He declared bankruptcy and spent the next 17 years of his life paying off the money he borrowed from friends to start his business.

- 1834: He was defeated for legislature again.

- 1835: He was engaged to be married, but his sweetheart died and his heart was broken.

- 1836: He had a nervous breakdown and spent the next six months in bed.

- 1838: He was defeated in becoming the speaker of the state legislature.

- 1840: He was defeated in becoming elector.

- 1843: He was defeated for Congress.

- 1846: He was defeated for Congress again.

- 1848: He was defeated for Congress a third time.

- 1849: He was rejected for the job of Land Officer in his home state.

- 1854: He stood for election for Senate and was defeated.

- 1856: He was defeated for Vice-President. He got less than 100 votes.

- 1858: He was defeated for Senate for the third time.

- 1860: He was elected President of the United States.

He did not stop trying. Why? I believe it was simply because he had hope that there was something better out there for him. It kept him going, and circumstances eventually gave in and he broke through.

STAY POSITIVE

Finally, brethren, whatsoever things are true, whatsoever things are honest, whatsoever things are just, whatsoever things are pure, whatsoever things are lovely, whatsoever things are of good report, if there be any virtue, and if there be any praise— think on these things (Philippians 4:8).

To be positive, you will have to start to see good in every event, every trial, and every challenge. Bad things may happen to you and you may not understand why, but believe that, as the Bible says, "All things work together for good to them that love God…" (Rom. 8:28).

Also, in staying positive, learn to thank God and give Him glory in everything. For the Bible says, "In everything give thanks: for this is the will of God in Christ Jesus concerning you" (1 Thess. 5:18). That was how Abraham kept going—he was positively minded, and he gave glory to God through his barrenness. He did not give thanks for being barren, but he thanked God that He was going to use his barrenness for His glory. He kept what God told him as his focus and did not focus on his circumstances.

And being not weak in faith, he considered not his own body now dead, when he was about an hundred years old, neither yet the deadness of Sarah's womb: he staggered not at the promise of God through unbelief; but was strong in faith, giving glory to God; and being fully persuaded that, what He had promised, He was able also to perform. And therefore it was imputed to him for righteousness (Romans 4:19-22).

Abraham, too, had reasons to yield to unbelief. He could have changed his mind regarding what he desired God to do for him. At some points in time, it seemed like the promise of God was never going to happen, but he gave God the glory all the same, confessing that God calls those things that were not as though they were (see Rom. 4:17).

In staying positive, know that God is in control of your destiny and that nothing happens to you without Him knowing about it. He will not allow you to experience anything that will not work out for your good, and He will not allow anything to happen to you which will have power over your destiny. No matter what happens, believe that you are who He says you are and walk like you know it. Do not think less of yourself and do not settle for anything less.

GET RID OF DREAM-KILLERS

Dream-killers are those in your life who are always complaining and always negative about your stand and conviction. They like to criticize your ideas, making you feel like you are inferior and will never make it. You do not need such people around you.

You need people who are positive; people who inspire you and challenge you to be your best. Not people who want to always prove that they know better. These people make you feel like you are not going to be able to achieve anything good. When you are down or are going through challenges, you need people who believe in your dreams, who know your potentials, and who will encourage you to keep going and not give up.

Have a plan, and plan to follow your plan. What I mean is, you need to ask yourself what things you need to do to achieve your goal in life. If you know the things to do, then you need to keep doing them even if you have tried them before and failed. If you do not stop trying, you will not give up and you will still believe that what you are hoping for will happen.

The first indication of hopelessness is not trying. If you do not stop trying, you will keep hoping; if you keep hoping, you will keep trying. Do not just sit there doing nothing and expect for something to happen. Your hope will eventually die out. When you do nothing, you show that you expect nothing. Nothing happens when you don't take action.

DEAL WITH FEAR

For ye have not received the spirit of bondage again to fear; but ye have received the Spirit of adoption, whereby we cry, Abba, Father (Romans 8:15).

One of the things the enemy will use against your expectations in life is fear. Fear can be a stronghold and very damaging, and I would like to share a bit more on this. Fear is a spirit, and it is not of God. Fear is a tool of the devil, and every believer must live above fear. Fear is the sense of insecurity or the feeling or anticipation that something bad is going to happen. People's fears are many. Some people are afraid of the enemy, satan and his agents, death, failing, getting cancer, losing their loved ones, the house burning down, having a car accident, flying, the future, old age, the dark, staying alone, being molested or raped, divorce, rejection, losing their jobs—you name it, some people live in fear of it.

You cannot live in fear and be completely safe, free from calamity or harm, and prospering. Fear is a horrible spirit no matter what form it takes. Fear—that you are never going to be able to achieve your goal, that you may not become what you think, that your prayers might not be answered, that your life will get worse, and that you may become a laughingstock—can kill your enthusiasm about the future. We all need to deal with fear; it happens to everybody. Fear is an enemy; it has a way of killing our expectations and taking the joy of living out of us if we let it. God said not to fear.

Fear thou not; for I am with thee: be not dismayed; for I am thy God: I will strengthen thee; yea, I will help thee; yea, I will uphold thee with the right hand of My righteousness. Behold, all they that were incensed against thee shall be ashamed and confounded: they shall be as nothing; and they that strive with thee shall perish. Thou shalt seek them, and shalt not find them, even them that contended with thee: they that war against thee shall be as nothing, and as a thing of nought. For I the Lord thy God will hold thy right hand, saying unto thee, Fear not; I will help thee (Isaiah 41:10-13).

To not fear means to learn to trust God, to have a sense of safety, to believe His Word, and act on it like you know it will not fail you. You see, fear is the opposite of faith. Faith in God drives out fear. Faith in God is understanding that the presence of God is always present with you. It is the sense of safety and the assurance of destiny. To experience total victory, we must be people of faith. People of faith conquer fear.

THE EFFECTS OF FEAR

Fear hinders God working in your life. It is a demonstration of lack of trust in God. Without faith it is impossible to please God. You cannot trust God with your life and still live in fear.

But without faith it is impossible to please Him: for he that cometh to God must believe that He is, and that He is a Rewarder of them that diligently seek Him (Hebrews 11:6).

Fear destroys your capacity to think positively. You cannot think straight when engrossed in your fears. Your thinking affects your behavior; when you are full of fear, you cannot think clearly. Fear and soundness of mind do not go together. Any decision made out of fear is likely to fail.

For God hath not given us the spirit of fear; but of power, and of love, and of a sound mind (2 Timothy 1:7).

Fear leads to indecision. Some people are afraid of making decisions—their lives are only going in circles, they are not moving forward, and they are not making any meaningful progress. They are afraid to take a bold step. They are afraid to take any risk. Why are they afraid? They fear that it is not going to work and they think that they are risking everything, but all they need to do is to go for it.

Fear reduces your capacity and potential to achieve. You cannot reach the height that God wants you to rise to if you allow fear in your life. Fear has killed many people's dreams, motivation, or will power. It has stopped some people from leaving their jobs even though it was the right thing to do; from changing their career even though it would be more fulfilling; from starting their own business even though they have what it takes; or from investing their savings. There are people who have thousands in their savings account and they just want to leave it there, even though it is not paying off, because they are afraid to take the risk. Fear has stopped many people from ending a relationship that will not lead anywhere, because they are afraid that they may never meet anybody again. Fear has also succeeded in stopping many people from marrying, because they think that nobody can be trusted. They cannot trust anybody because of what they have experienced in the past.

It is wrong to think that you cannot achieve something that you have not tried before. Until you try it, you do not know what ability you possess. It is always better to try and fail at something than to not try at all. You will discover that you are becoming more creative, more efficient, and more productive as you gain power over fears. You will start to view your world and your challenges differently, actually seeing some challenges as an opportunity to try something different. You will take risks and venture into new things, and they will take you to a higher level. Fear will keep you down, but confidence in yourself and in your God will lift you up.

Fear fosters torment. It is a thief of peace and joy. You cannot have the sense of safety and experience peace if you are under the power of fear. Fear is oppressive and depressive. An example is the fear of death.

There is no fear in love; but perfect love casteth out fear: because fear hath torment. He that feareth is not made perfect in love (1 John 4:18).

Can you imagine what fear does to some African people who cannot go to their home towns because of the fear of witchcraft, spirits, enemies, superstitions, and all that? I am African, and I see this torment all over the place among African people. I have seen people who cannot drive in good cars or do anything which would make them appear to be living in prosperity because they are afraid their enemies will get jealous and attack them. Isn't that torment? I have seen people who won't announce it when they or their wives become pregnant or when they get promoted at work or when their children gain admission into university because they fear what their "enemy" will think. Fear is bondage and torment; you are never free if you do not kill it!

Fear damages your capacity to trust people and enjoy relationship with them. A lot of us are afraid to be around people because we do not want to be gossiped about, we do not want to be hurt again, et cetera. Perhaps you have been jilted or have divorced before and do not want to be hurt again. If you cannot trust again, develop new relationships, and start all over again—if you keep being afraid and allowing fear to have power over your life—you let it stand in the way of your destiny.

What you fear can happen to you. Just as faith attracts God to our situation, fear opens up our lives to evil. Faith gives God permission to access your life, and fear gives the devil that same permission. Faith is God's environment for miracles; fear is the devil's environment for torment. God cannot operate where there is fear, and satan will have a field day where God cannot operate.

I also will choose their delusions, and will bring their fears upon them; because when I called, none did answer; when I spake, they did not hear: but they did evil before Mine eyes, and chose that in which I delighted not (Isaiah 66:4).

OVERCOMING FEAR

Admit your fears and confess them before God. We sometimes think that we will be less spiritual if we let God or others know about our fears. But God knows us very well, and He understands our frailties and the weakness of our bodies. He will never condemn you for being honest with Him. God is not only interested in your faith; He is also interested in your fears and wants to help you. He is an ever-present help in times of trouble.

> *For we do not have a High Priest who cannot sympathize with our weaknesses, but was in all points tempted as we are, yet without sin. Let us therefore come boldly to the throne of grace, that we may obtain mercy and find grace to help in time of need* (Hebrews 4:15-16 NKJV).

He who admits his faults shall prosper. Healing starts only when we admit our problems and table them before God. You may also need to talk to someone. Do not hold all the anxieties and fears inside. Share them with somebody who can pray with you and cast out that evil spirit. Remember, fear is a spirit.

Confess the sins in your life, if there are any. Sometimes fear and anxiety come as a result of one's own sin and guilt. If you have committed a sin or done anything evil, your fear and anxiety are probably God or your own conscience trying to get your attention. You need to repent, confess your sin, seek God's forgiveness, and set things right with God.

> *My little children, these things write I unto you, that ye sin not. And if any man sin, we have an advocate with the Father, Jesus Christ the righteous: and He is the propitiation for our sins: and not for ours only, but also for the sins of the whole world* (1 John 2:1-2).

We reinforce our sense of righteousness when we receive forgiveness and become bold in the face of the enemy. That is why the Bible says the wicked flees when no one pursues him, but the righteous are as bold as a lion (see Prov. 28:1).

Focus on Jesus. The Bible says that our sufficiency is of God (see 2 Cor. 3:5). One of the keys to dealing with fear is to fix our focus on the Person of Jesus Christ. When all of your concentration is on yourself, you are likely to focus on your family history, your lack of the right qualifications, your nationality, your mistakes, your ignorance, and so on. What you see in yourself can either make you proud or it can make you afraid. Either way, you are open to the devil.

When all you see is your lack in the face of challenges, you are always going to fear. The fact is that in life you are sometimes going to face something that seems bigger than you can handle. If in the midst of that you can see Jesus, you will not fear.

Know the presence of God. Knowing that God watches over you and will never leave you can minister grace and strength to you. This knowledge will embolden you in the midst of adversity. He promised that He would never leave nor forsake us. You are never alone. He will stand by you through thick and thin and will not let anything destroy you. You can know His presence wherever you are. Never think you are all by yourself, because your Maker is with you. Your Father God, the One who says you will make it despite the odds, is always with you. He says:

Fear thou not; for I am with thee: be not dismayed; for I am thy God: I will strengthen thee; yea, I will help thee; yea, I will uphold thee with the right hand of My righteousness…. For I the Lord thy God will hold thy right hand, saying unto thee, Fear not; I will help thee (Isaiah 41:10,13).

You will need to feed on the Word daily. The Word gives the believer the correct perspective of who He really is and what His end will be like. The entrance of the Word gives light and understanding to the simple. It is not what the doctor says or your family history that matters, it is what the Word says you are. You are who God says you are, and you will become who God says you will become. The more you feed your spirit with the Word, the more you are able to develop your spirit. Your spirit is able to subjugate the flesh when it is developed. Fear is of the flesh, and you fear more when you are in the flesh. When you are in the spirit, fear will lose its grip on you. Feed on the Word like your life depends on it. Feed on it daily and that fighting spirit inside you will generate. Fear has no part in you; you have got to kill it!

VICTORY OVER THE SPIRIT OF DISCOURAGEMENT

If thou faint in the day of adversity, thy strength is small (Proverbs 24:10).

We can all experience discouragement in life because, as we all know, life is full of ups and downs. The devil often uses the circumstances we go through to stand in our way and hinder what we are seeking to achieve. Discouragement is one of the reasons why many people today are living in frustration and are unhappy in life. It is one of the reasons people cannot take the initiative to try something new. Many people have quit schools, quit jobs, ended their career, closed down businesses, and even divorced. In addition, because of discouragement many have resorted to drugs and alcohol and some have even committed or attempted suicide.

Discouragement can happen to anybody, no matter your anointing or achievements in life. Elijah, one of the greatest prophets who lived, also experienced discouragement and asked God to end his life (see 1 Kings 19:1-4). Many years ago, a distant cousin of mine attempted suicide by taking poison. He had lost his job and borrowed some money and invested it into a business, but the business collapsed and the lenders wanted their money and he could not pay it back. So he thought the best way to end it was to take poison and die.

Perhaps you are reading this book and are thinking about doing something like this because you feel frustrated, tired, betrayed, and fed up with your present situation. I would like to tell you not to let that demon knock you down, and I want you to know that you are not the only one to experience this. Other people have had the same experiences and they broke through. You, too, can break through. The Bible says, "And let us not be weary in well doing: for in due season we shall reap, if we faint not" (Gal. 6:9). Do not give up yet!

The nearer the miracle, the more challenging and painful it gets sometimes. You cannot tell, but it is likely that your breakthrough is just around the corner. If you are reading this book, I would like to announce to you that your due season has come! You cannot afford to faint now.

SYMPTOMS OF DISCOURAGEMENT

1. Worry—When you are starting to lose your peace and cannot enjoy sleep like before. When your confidence or assurance that something great is ahead is starting to wane.

2. Slackness—When you are starting to get fed up, you have lost your initiative, you are not excited about life anymore, and you are not excited about your job anymore. When you struggle to wake up, dress up, and resume work like before.

3. Loss of passion—When your fire and zeal is dying out. When you expected things to work out in a certain way with a particular thing and they do not. As a result you are starting to reconsider your expectations.

4. Self-pity—When you become too conscious of your weaknesses and limitations and are starting to feel sorry for yourself. You think nobody really understands or cares about you. You begin to think that you are the only one going through what you are going through, and you are wondering and asking, "Why me, Lord? What did I do wrong?"

5. Lack of motivation—You do not see any reason why you should carry on, and you need somebody to talk you into doing what was once your routine and your passion. You are starting to lose your sense of purpose.

6. Complaints—You are starting to notice what is wrong with the system, and the lapses are more obvious than before. It appears that all the people around you are making too many mistakes and often seem to be getting

everything wrong. You are starting to make a big deal out of things that had not bothered you before.

7. Excuses—You are coming up with reasons why you think something will not work even though you have not tried it before. You try to justify your lack of interest in a thing, even though it is needful and you know it is your responsibility and duty to get it done or completed.

8. Blaming culture—You do not want to take responsibility for your situation. You want to blame it on the system, on your family background, or on your parents. You suddenly discover that you were abused as a child.

9. Procrastination—You cannot get yourself to do a task now; you want to leave it till tomorrow. Somewhere on the inside of you there is fear that it might not work out, so you put it off. There is also fear that you will not get it right.

10. Aggression—You are easily upset. Little things make you angry, although you were not like that before.

11. Inferiority complex—You are starting to feel inadequate and less than your contemporaries. You find yourself allowing your challenges to overshadow and suppress your past achievements and your potential. Your challenge is making you forget who you really are and the ability God has given you.

12. Self-rejection—You do not look after yourself the way you did before. You no longer want to go out, and you are starting to keep away from important social meetings. You may also not be eating well like you used to. You now have tendencies to feed more on junk, under- or over-eating. You do not care to wash, wear perfume or cologne, and look good. Perhaps you are also starting to have thoughts of harming yourself in some way.

You do not have to see all of the above happening to you to know that discouragement is trying to get to you. It suffices if you want to do something about it after identifying only one of them. Discouragement is of the devil; he wants to make you feel like a loser, give up your hope, and stop fighting for it. He knows that if he can only get you to faint, he is able to hinder your destiny.

People do not get discouraged over nothing. Situations they find themselves in bring them to that point. The devil likes to take advantage of such situations in order to take somebody out of God's purpose for his life. We are more prone to attack in certain situations than in others. You need to know which situations the devil will want to use to attack you. When you familiarize yourself with these situations, you are in a better place to disallow him from discouraging you.

THE ENVIRONMENT FOR DISCOURAGEMENT

Satan may be a liar, but he is not stupid. He will not attack you with discouragement during your happy moments. In saying this, I mean when you have just got a new job, bought a new house, changed your car, just got married, or just won the lottery. He may attack you with pride but not with discouragement. The devil will not attack you with discouragement when things are working out beautifully for you, because he knows that will not work. However, there are times when you are more prone to experience discouragement.

1. It appears you are failing despite your hard work. Sometimes things just don't work out the way you want, despite everything you put into it. It can be challenging when you read very hard for an examination and you do not pass it, when you invest a lot of money and time into a venture and it doesn't yield any dividend, or when you put your all into a relationship and it seems to be failing. It can be very challenging when you have done all you need to do and yet there is nothing to show for it. It is discouraging, isn't it?

2. You persistently suffer defeat in one particular area. It can be discouraging if you fail a particular exam and have to retake it several times, when you lose in a fight against a bad habit and are relapsing, or when you fail your driving

test after trying a few times. It is easy to give up on the idea of marriage if you've been with a few people but nothing good came out of it. You will need guts to start all over again. It can be tough to carry on trying for a baby if you have been to see the doctor several times and the outcome is always negative.

3. You are experiencing delay in the fulfillment of an expectation. You had always thought that you would be married by twenty-five, but you are now thirty-five and nothing is happening. You thought you would not have to pray and fast to have a baby after marriage, but doctors are telling you what you do not want to hear. You thought you would be starting on a new job just after graduation, but it is over one year now since you graduated from the university and you are still believing God for a job. You sowed a seed of faith; you paid tithes but you are still waiting. Yes, it is the environment for discouragement. It sounded like going overseas would make things better, but you are now starting to wonder whether you made the right decision. Hope deferred makes the heart sick (see Prov. 13:12).

4. Things just go wrong and it is not your fault. Sometimes things happen that we don't have control over and there is nothing we can do about it. For example, the sudden collapse of a company, the sudden death of a loved one, the worsening situation of somebody you are praying for, or a strong pillar in your congregation leaving town or the church when you were counting on him to help with something.

5. Your colleagues or friends are making progress while you are stagnant or retrogressing. God has a different plan for everybody and works differently with everybody. And life has a way of responding to us differently, too. Sometimes people you start out with move faster and achieve more than you have. Life is full of that. The devil is very good at pointing people to their friends who have gone ahead of them. He does that not to challenge them to work harder, but

in order to break their spirit and make them lose confidence in their ability and feel like losers. It can be challenging for you to see people you have started out with or people you helped to start out in life doing better than you while you are stuck. The devil will easily make you believe you are under curses if you let him. The devil is a liar.

6. God gives you a new opportunity, a new challenge, or a new position. To be thrown into an opportunity that you never expected has the tendency to overwhelm you, and the devil can use that for discouragement. I know this is not common to most people; a lot will become proud instead. But a few can be attacked with discouragement at this point. During this period, the devil will want to make you feel inadequate or inferior to the challenge before you. He will want you to compare yourself with people who put on those shoes before you, especially if they were very good. He will want to make you think that you have not got enough knowledge, exposure, strength, or money to make it happen. But remember, the Bible says, "…by strength shall no man prevail" (1 Sam. 2:9).

7. You are going through rejection. I have seen that people come and go in life. Sometimes the people you count on most just leave when you need them most. The experience of rejection can be very challenging, and the devil uses it all the time. You are likely to feel rejected when people you count on are leaving, or when the person who once told you he loves you and will spend the rest of his life with you walks away or is seen with somebody else. People have become mentally ill, have attempted suicide, and some have even killed themselves because of rejection.

8. As a pastor, you can feel it when the people you pray and fast for are turning against you. When people are falsely discussing what they know nothing about or ganging up with others to stand in your way. You feel it when you are going through challenges and the people you thought would be there for you are attacking you. You feel alone

when you need somebody but they are not there for you. But know that when men forget you, God will not forget you (see Isa. 43:1-5; 49:14-16). Always remember that you are never alone—He will never abandon you.

OVERCOME DISCOURAGEMENT

Never lose sight of God's promises. By now you must have discovered that things do not always happen as we want them to. Sometimes it is going to be tough and difficult, because the Bible says, "Many are the afflictions of the righteous" (Ps. 34:19). No matter the ups and downs you experience, just keep His promises in focus and do not lose sight of them. Since you know that, "His promises are yea and amen," as long as you can see them, you will have the strength to keep fighting and waiting for the promise to be fulfilled (2 Cor. 1:20). If the devil cannot make you set aside what you know from the Word, he cannot stop you.

I speak into your life that that devil cannot stop you. No matter what you are going through, you are going to hold on until you break through. You will break through as the Bible says, "…Thou shalt make thy way prosperous, and then thou shalt have good success" (Josh. 1:8). As you hold on to that word you have received, meditate and act on it.

Never accept defeat or lack as your portion. Know that God has a plan for you, and His plans for you will always come to pass, no matter what. Never accept anything to the contrary as your portion. Know that challenging situations are going to arise—because we know that things do not always work out as we want them to—but they are not your final destination or your ultimate end. They are only a means to your destiny in God. It may be difficult when you have to face such circumstances, but it is not going to be permanent—you are going to come out.

For which cause we faint not; but though our outward man perish, yet the inward man is renewed day by day. For our light affliction, which is but for a moment, worketh for us a far more exceeding and eternal weight of glory; while we look not at the

42

*things which are seen, but at the things which are not seen: for
the things which are seen are temporal; but the things which are
not seen are eternal* (2 Corinthians 4:16-18).

When you find yourself having to go through difficult times, know
that it is a passage, not your portion. Do not accept it. See that you are
an overcomer, declare it by faith, and act like you know it is so.

Learn to encourage yourself in the Lord. To be a fighter and a
winner, you must learn how to encourage yourself without counting
on anybody. Sometimes you are going to find yourself in a situation
where you have to stand and fight alone because no one else
understands why you have to do it, and no one will understand why
you must hold on to something that is not working. Sometimes people
are going to blame you for your problems. And you know, sometimes
people get tired of people, too. You must learn to stand alone and
encourage yourself. That was what David did when he was in distress,
"...David encouraged himself in the Lord his God" (1 Sam. 30:6).

Encourage yourself by reminding yourself who God has made you
in Christ. The Bible says, "...who hath blessed us with all spiritual
blessings in heavenly places in Christ" (Eph. 1:3). You are blessed no
matter what.

> *I can do all things through Christ who strengthens me* (Philippians
> 4:13 NKJV).

> *Nay, in all these things we are more than conquerors through
> Him that loved us* (Romans 8:37).

In Christ, God says you are triumphant—you are an overcomer
(see 2 Cor. 2:14; 1 John 4:4). Speak those words out loud to yourself and
make the devil nervous. The Bible says that Christ has been made unto us
wisdom, righteousness, sanctification, and redemption (see 1 Cor. 1:30).
This means that because you have Christ in you, you are no fool. Christ
in you is your gift of wisdom. You can make it; you will make it. I urge
you—do not let the devil intimidate you.

Now say to yourself, "Because I have Christ in me, I have wisdom. I am full of understanding; my mind is blessed. I can do all things through Christ who strengthens me."

Understand the seasons of change. Whatever God does will be in His own time and in its own season. Ecclesiastes says that there is an appointed time for everything God has promised (see Eccles. 3:1). Whatever you are going through now is only working out a blessing for you (see Rom. 8:28). It may be tough for you now, and it may appear as if things are not working according to God's plan. Well, if you can only hold on, in due time and season God will make good His promises for you and show you He is not a liar (see Hab. 2:2-3). Just because it has not happened yet does not mean that it will not—it is only a matter of time. Allow the process to take its course. Nothing has changed—God has not changed and His word for you has not changed. I see God's word coming to pass in your life if you hold on. It is only a matter of time.

Learn to rebuke the demon of discouragement. Remember, discouragement is a demon. It attacks everybody—the rich, the poor, the successful, the failure, the single, the married, the employed, and the unemployed. Remember, satan wants you to stop trying—he wants you to end that relationship, quit that job, or walk away from that church. He wants to interrupt God's purpose for your life, he wants to kill your destiny, and he wants you to kill yourself. Discouragement is a spirit you must learn to confront.

The Bible says that you shall resist the devil and he shall flee (see James 4:7). It also says, "Whosoever shall say unto this mountain, Be thou removed, and be thou cast into the sea; and shall not doubt in his heart...he shall have whatsoever he saith" (see Mark 11:23). Shut that devil up! He is a liar. Tell him, "Get behind me satan! I am who God says I am."

Keep confessing what you believe the Word of God has said about you. What God has planned for you will come to pass. God's Word will never fall to the ground. The things that you are going through have no power over your destiny. You need to maintain that knowledge, and you need to keep declaring that it is so, no matter what.

If the devil cannot close your mouth—if you will continue to declare it—he can't stop your manifestation. The Bible says that death and life are in the power of the tongue (see Prov. 18:21). What you say is what you will become. Keep speaking the word you have received; speak it until it becomes life and spirit in you, until it takes form, and until it manifests in you. Remember, the devil is a liar; you are who God says you are.

THE JOY OF THE LORD

Do not let the devil steal your joy. The Bible says in Nehemiah 8:10 that the joy of the Lord is your strength. It also says in Philippians 4: 4 that you should rejoice always, and we are urged in Ephesians 5:20 to give thanks to God the Father in all things. Do not let the devil steal your heart of joy and gratitude. If the devil can take away the joy of the Lord in you, he is able to destroy your strength.

Joy is very fundamental in overcoming the spirit of discouragement. There are two kinds of joy—the worldly type and joy in the Holy Spirit, or the joy of the Lord. Worldly joy is about being happy and it is born out of good things happening. However, the joy of the Lord is spiritual excitement, a feeling of contentment, and the fire and energy that makes you want to keep going with something, even when there are no physical indications that things will go right. Joy is different from happiness. Happiness is the feeling of pleasure or satisfaction that is born out of achievement, events, or good occurrences, while joy does not depend on any outside event. It is satisfaction on the inside.

> *Although the fig tree shall not blossom, neither shall fruit be in the vines; the labor of the olive shall fail, and the fields shall yield no meat; the flock shall be cut off from the fold, and there shall be no herd in the stalls: yet I will rejoice in the Lord, I will joy in the God of my salvation* (Habakkuk 3:17-18).

Joy is the spiritual excitement that energizes you to keep on going, despite the odds, because of the hope of glory. This joy comes from the Holy Spirit. Joy is an important criterion for anybody trying overcome trials or obstacles in life and to reach a desired destiny. If satan, the enemy, can steal one's joy, he can get him to be depressed, quit school, quit his job, move out of town, end relationships, or even commit suicide. The joy you have in something is what can keep you going even when it becomes challenging. Without joy inside you, you will live a sad life. Without joy nothing motivates you, and without motivation in life, you are not going to be a fighter. It was joy that kept Jesus going despite the challenge of the Cross. Joy ignited by the hope of glory was the strength which kept pulling Him on (see Heb. 12:2-3).

Each one of us needs the joy of the Lord to go through life in view of the challenges that we encounter. Our joy in the Lord is indeed our place of safety. If we lose this joy we lose the passion for life, we become depressed, we become suicidal, and we become unproductive in our work. When we lose the joy of relationship, we want to separate from people who care about us. Do not let the devil steal your joy.

SUSTAINING JOY

Put your trust in God. You ought to trust that nothing will happen to you without God knowing about it. Trust that God will not allow anything to come your way except what will work out for your good (see Rom. 8:28). Trust that in Him your future or destiny is secured. If you can only put your trust in God, you will not worry about anything or be anxious. The truth is that what you cannot handle, God can.

Do not allow your challenges to overwhelm you. Focus on Jesus, His faithfulness and power to deliver, and what He has done in your life. Keep on trusting Him, and joy will rise from the inside of you like a spring. Your destiny is not dependent on your situation. Your life is in God's hands, and He is working out something for you. It is only a matter of time. I encourage you to rejoice in the Lord always.

Understand God's purpose for your life. Many a time we find ourselves in unnecessary hardship because we are doing what God has not called us to do.

Do not take on a project you are not sure is God's will for you. Do not chase after things that God is not giving you. Do not let worldly things have a hold on you, and do not chase them like your happiness depends on them. Do not keep hurts; learn to forgive everything even before it happens. Do not be too concerned about what people think of you. Make the Bible your standard and learn to be good to everyone.

Anything God has mapped out for you will work out for you. You have got to believe that. You will find that your joy is in what God has assigned for you. God will give you joy in doing exactly what is His will for you, even when things are not working out as you thought they would. A lack of joy for something may be an indication that either you are not called to it or that you are not trusting God to handle it for you.

Walk with vision. Learn to put your focus and your attention more on what God has shown you as your destiny. It can be rough sometimes on your journey there, but if what you are passing through now cannot blur the future, you will not be hindered.

> *While we look not at the things which are seen, but at the things which are not seen: for the things which are seen are temporal; but the things which are not seen are eternal* (2 Corinthians 4:18).

Learn to give God thanks in everything and for everything. We must make this a lifestyle. We must give thanks no matter what happens. The joy of the Lord is released in the place of prayer and thanksgiving (see 1 Thess. 5:18). Thanksgiving releases joy and overcomes depression. It produces hope and vision. When you do not give thanks and rejoice in the Lord, you quench the Holy Spirit inside you. When you quench Him, you put a hindrance on the work of the Holy Spirit. When you hinder Him, you start to feel inadequate and unworthy, and your challenges start to overwhelm you. You must learn to give thanks in all things, even when things are not going as you initially thought they would.

THE POWER OF EXPECTATION AND YOUR DESTINY

Expectation is very powerful and has a bearing on destiny. A believer must be full of expectations in life.

The Lord is good unto them that wait for Him, to the soul that seeketh Him. It is good that a man should both hope and quietly wait for the salvation of the Lord (Lamentations 3:25-26).

Expectation is when you are waiting for something to happen. It is good to hope for something. The opposite of expectation is despondency. Your expectation defines the quality of your life. It defines what you will have in the future. When you expect nothing, nothing happens. When you expect to fail, you become an underachiever. It is good to have expectations, but is better to have positive expectations. Without a positive expectation in life, you live a sad life, become depressed, worry over nothing, you may even become suicidal. Positive expectation is what makes you alive, passionate, determined, and productive.

Faith is about expectations. If you are walking in faith, you've got to expect something to happen. If you are acting on the word of God spoken into your life, expect results. If you are sowing seed, expect the harvest. Faith in God makes a believer do something—faith in the assurance of His integrity and in His ability and power to make good His word—but it is the expectation of the believer that sustains what he has done in faith. It is his expectation that creates the factory that manufactures the future or brings the harvest. The believer's expectation releases the anointing to make something happen. When he expects nothing, nothing happens. And usually people do nothing when they are expecting nothing. You see, expectation is powerful. Through expectation:

- You develop joy for living and are excited about tomorrow.

- You overcome fear and will never, ever dream of killing yourself. People kill themselves because they lost all hope and life has lost its meaning to them.

- You are empowered to be a fighter, you are able to endure, and obstacles don't deter you.

- You are able to pay the price and make uncommon sacrifices, because you know it will birth something. You don't go all out for something if you aren't sure something good can come out of it. Some people don't see the need to sow seed because they don't understand the power of harvest.

- Present circumstances don't suppress you.

- Your eyes will be on the future, and you will walk with the future in mind.

- You can know that your life is heading somewhere, and this makes you bold and confident about yourself.

- Life is a journey; every new day comes with its package. There is something that God is cooking for you, and it is part of your destiny—it's bound to happen, satan can't kill it, and you expect it.

RENEWING YOUR EXPECTATIONS

Now we know that our expectations don't always happen at the time we think they will. Expectations can be delayed, and when your expectations are delayed you can become sick and want to give up. You've got to learn to keep trusting God and keep expecting something good to happen to you no matter what. Here are some steps for practicing this.

Meditate in the Word daily. Keep feeding on the Word; keep picturing your life and future in light of it. Don't allow anything to keep you from the Word.

Recall what God did for you in the past. Remember, He healed you before, He can heal you again. If He protected you before, He can again. What He did before, He can do for you again.

Learn to just praise in the midst of all. Remember, if the devil can't steal your joy, he can't stop you. Keep praising the Lord; rejoice in Him always.

Confess what you are hoping for. Keep declaring it until it comes to pass—there is power in your words.

Continue to sow a seed of faith toward it. From time to time, you need to take an offering and thank God for it because you believe it. Let your offering reach God for a memorial.

Chapter Two

The Integrity of God

Then the Lord came down in the cloud and stood there with him and proclaimed His name, the Lord. And He passed in front of Moses, proclaiming, "The Lord, the Lord, the compassionate and gracious God, slow to anger, abounding in love and faithfulness, maintaining love to thousands, and forgiving wickedness, rebellion and sin. Yet He does not leave the guilty unpunished; He punishes the children and their children for the sin of the fathers to the third and fourth generation." Moses bowed to the ground at once and worshiped (Exodus 34:5-8 NIV).

When Moses said to the Lord, "Show me Your glory," he was, in essence, saying to God, "Reveal Yourself to me that I may know You, encounter You, and experience You deeper and at a level I have not known You before" (Exod. 33:18 NIV). God answers Moses' prayer, but we see that God did not show him some huge and gigantic personality who is covered in bright light. What did God show Moses? He showed him the awesomeness of His name, His compassionate and gracious nature, His heart of love, and His ability to forgive sin. He showed him the God of covenant and judgment, and He showed him His faithfulness and integrity.

We all need to have a personal revelation of God. We all need to discover God for ourselves. There is a lot about God that we need to discover. Our relationship with God should not be based on what others have told us but on our revelation of Him. So, like Moses, our prayer should be, "Lord, help me know You more. Show me Your glory." There is a lot about God that a believer needs to discover.

Our revelation of God will impact our character and our relationship with God and with people. The names of God reveal to us who God is; from His names we can discover His attributes. We can discover His power and His might. For instance, He is:

- Elohim—strong one and divine

- Adonai—Lord, indicating the Master over all

- El Elyon—most high, the strongest one

- El Roi—the strong one who sees

- El Shaddai—almighty God

- El Olam—everlasting God

- Yahweh—Lord "I Am," meaning the eternal, self-existent God

From His holiness we know that He can never do anything sinful or wrong. Knowing His heart of love shows us that He can never hate us. As a judge we know that He will never tolerate evil. By His integrity and faithfulness, we know that God is honest, reliable, and dependable. Knowing God and experiencing Him will make a lot of difference in our character. I am of the opinion that the level at which we can trust God will be dependent, not just on how much we know of His majestic power and His ability to do absolutely anything, but on how much we know about His integrity and faithfulness. You see, the integrity of a man is the most important thing about him—not his wealth, his power, his position, or his accomplishments. Your character is your glory and your honor. It is more important than riches.

A good name is rather to be chosen than great riches, and loving favor rather than silver and gold (Proverbs 22:1).

Also, the quality of any relationship that you will have with anybody will be determined by the level of trust that exists between you and that person. The character of the person you are in relationship with will determine how much you can trust him. If you cannot trust him enough, you cannot enjoy the best that the relationship can offer. In the same vein, how much you can enjoy from your relationship with God will be determined by how much you can trust Him. As such, your level of trust in God will be determined by how much you know of His integrity and faithfulness.

I believe that integrity is one of the most fundamental characteristics of God that every believer must be familiar with. Knowing the integrity of God will empower us to be able to trust Him and hold on to His Word until we see its fulfillment in our lives, no matter what we go through. God is trustworthy.

> *God is not a man, that He should lie; neither the son of man, that*
> *He should repent: hath He said, and shall He not do it? or hath*
> *He spoken, and shall He not make it good?* (Numbers 23:19)

When God makes promises, He fulfills them. Every promise of God in your life will be fulfilled in Jesus' name. One of the reasons why you must discover His faithfulness and integrity is because life can be full of challenges. Believers, too, go through discouraging times. Life is not always easy; sometimes things get tough and hard. Sometimes things do not work out as we expect, and sometimes it feels like God is not there and the Word of God is void of power. However, knowing God's promises and knowing that He is undeniably reliable and will never break His promises will keep us going even when things are rough. When everybody has deserted us, when the future looks bleak and it feels like God is very far, we will be assured of His love and care. We will be encouraged to keep on pressing on, because we know that He is faithful and whatever He has promised will ultimately come to pass.

> *Know therefore that the Lord thy God, He is God, the faithful*
> *God, which keepeth covenant and mercy with them that love*
> *Him and keep His commandments to a thousand generations*
> (Deuteronomy 7:9).

I speak into your life, and I say He will do it. I say He will do everything He has said concerning you in Jesus' name. Every word of God you are standing on will come to pass in your life.

WHY SOME PROMISES DO NOT COME TO PASS

Some things do not happen because of the law of harvest.

Do not be deceived: God cannot be mocked. A man reaps what he sows (Galatians 6:7 NIV).

If you are holding on to God's Word for something that He has promised in His Word and you are faithful to Him and living right with Him, I would like you to know that, though your situation might not be right at the moment, you will come through it. God will glorify Himself in your situation. But if you do not have regard for God and you are never faithful to Him, then know that you do not have the right to claim His promises. It is the law of harvest—do not expect what you have not sown. If you want God to honor Himself in your life, you must honor God first.

Wherefore the Lord God of Israel saith, I said indeed that thy house, and the house of thy father, should walk before Me for ever: but now the Lord saith, Be it far from Me; for them that honor Me I will honor, and they that despise Me shall be lightly esteemed (1 Samuel 2:30).

You honor Him by giving Him His due place in your life, in all your affairs, and by obeying His Word and living right. Also, you honor God when you demonstrate that you love Him more than what you have— when you are willing and able to lay down anything for Him. His Word says, "Honor the Lord with thy substance, and with the firstfruits of all thine increase" (Prov. 3:9).

To honor God with your substance means to treat everything that you have as less important than God and to use what you have to serve Him. Do not treat your offerings and tithes as a way of getting God to bless you. Treat them instead as your way of showing to God that you recognize Him as your Lord, your Provider, and the Source of all your increase. That way, you honor Him. If you treat your offerings and tithes as a way of honoring God, you will give your best, and you will give cheerfully, lavishly, and with reverence.

Some promises and prophecies of God come with conditions, dependent on certain requirements for them to come to pass. When we do not meet those conditions, those promises do not come to pass. A good example of this is in the story of Elijah and the widow of Zarephat (see 1 Kings 17:11-16). Now just think about it—what would have become of Elijah's words to the widow if she had jeered at the prophet and walked away? Another good example of promises that come with a condition is in the story of Elisha and Naaman (see 2 Kings 5:1,9-14). Naaman would never have been cured if he had not dipped in the River Jordan as commanded by Elisha.

Consider also the story of Jesus and the man born blind (see John 9:1-11). This man came back seeing only after he acted on what Jesus said for him to do. The condition for him seeing was to go and wash, not in just any pool, but in the pool of Siloam. It did not make any sense; there was nothing scientific about it, and possibly the blind man had never heard of anyone receiving sight by washing clay off his eyes, but he believed the word Jesus said. As he complied with the instruction, the anointing came on him and broke that yoke, and he could see. Nothing would have happened if he had washed in another pool. If you can comply with what God says to do, anything is possible.

The Lord requires that we demonstrate faith in Him and in His Word. When we do not demonstrate faith, we hinder the fulfillment of His promises in our lives.

> *Let us therefore fear, lest, a promise being left us of entering into His rest, any of you should seem to come short of it. For unto us was the gospel preached, as well as unto them: but the word preached did not profit them, not being mixed with faith in them that heard it* (Hebrews 4:1-2).

You have to accept what He says by faith and act on His words like they are so in order to see the Word come to pass in your life. Without faith, nothing happens. Faith means to accept that what God has said about you is so and that it will happen as He has said it. Faith also means the ability to stand on the Word of God and act on it as if it is so, no matter the circumstances you find yourself in, and to continue to do so until that Word happens.

THE TRIAL OF FAITH

Your faith in God and in His Word is always going to be tried. A time will come when you will feel like God is not real or He has forsaken you. You will certainly experience a rough time, because challenges are part of life and Christians go through them as well.

> *That ye be not slothful, but followers of them who through faith and patience inherit the promises. For when God made promise to Abraham, because He could swear by no greater, He sware by Himself, saying, Surely blessing I will bless thee, and multiplying I will multiply thee. And so, after he had patiently endured, he obtained the promise* (Hebrews 6:12-15).

Abraham went through some rough times before the promise was fulfilled. When that situation comes, the devil will want to take advantage of it to make you doubt the Word of God and turn your back against His promises. That rough-time experience is called the trial of faith. Your determination and willingness to endure what you have to go through at that time will be the proof that you actually have faith in what God has said.

VIRTUES OF FAITH

> *And beside this, giving all diligence, add to your faith virtue; and to virtue knowledge* (2 Peter 1:5).

We have said that faith, in simple terms, means accepting that what God has said is so. We also need works to make our faith a living faith. The virtues of faith are necessary in making faith alive and active. The word "virtue" means behavior that shows a high moral standard or a lifestyle that is considered good and desirable. The virtues of faith, therefore, have to do with having a lifestyle of faith. In other words, virtues of faith show the behavior of the man who is walking in the faith of God. Some of these virtues are:

- Faith determination
- Persistence of faith
- Patience of faith
- Endurance of faith
- Temperance of faith
- Joy of faith

FAITH DETERMINATION

Determination is where the mind is set on achieving something, no matter the cost or challenges. Determination insists on succeeding in a thing even when it physically looks impossible. It is the courage to confront one's challenges and not give up, the mindset that does not accept "no" for an answer. Determination is birthed out of a conviction that something can be done and must be done. A man of faith sticks to his conviction, even when things are not going according to plan and there are challenges. You know a man of faith by how he responds to difficulty. A man of faith does not give up in difficulty. He holds on to his conviction, even when it is not comfortable and there is no physical indication that something will happen.

If you have faith in God for something—if your faith is built in His Word—it will generate determination in you, and you will not stop until what you believe God for comes through. As a matter of fact, you will be willing to do anything and go to any extent to see the manifestation of what you are trusting God for. An example of this kind of determination is the woman with the issue of blood (see Mark 5:25-34). She was willing to violate the norms and customs we see in Leviticus (see

Lev. 15:25-26). She disregarded the frailties of her body and pushed through the crowd and touched Jesus.

Do you remember when David first appeared on the battle scene, when Goliath defied the army of Israel? (See 1 Samuel 17:22-38.) He was resisted by his older brother when he intended to confront Goliath, the giant. Even King Saul was of the opinion that David did not have what it would take to kill the giant, but no one, not even the king, could stop David because he believed that God could save Israel through him.

Life is full of obstacles and challenges. The devil will want to use anything to stand in your way and prevent you from fulfilling your purpose. If only you can maintain your stand and keep pressing on, you will always achieve what you set out to.

Remember, there is such a thing as the trial of faith. The fact that you have faith does not mean that things will happen automatically for you. Despite your faith, trouble and some hard times may come. If you will not be discouraged, if you will not settle on defeat, and if you will not leave the outcome to chance but fight for it, your miracle will not be stopped. To keep on despite all the odds, you will need determination. With determination of faith, you will be on the winning side. You might miss it sometimes and you might fall, but if you can only rise up and press on, you will get to your destiny.

PERSISTENCE OF FAITH

Faith is persistent, and "persistence" means to continue firmly in a course of action in spite of difficulty or opposition. Persistence is a product of determination. When you are determined to succeed in something, you will keep on pursuing success in that thing, no matter what, until you get to where you are targeting. The blind man, Bartimaeus, the woman with the issue of blood, and David when he decided to kill Goliath are also good examples of persistence. Another story that demonstrates persistence is the widow before the unjust judge (see Luke 18:1-8).

The steps you take and your actions after opposition, resistance, difficulties, or failure are a revelation of what you believe in. They reveal your conviction and the level of your faith. You may need to apply for that particular job in that same company ten times—just go on and do it. That is persistence. You may need to try and try again for your degree, but that should not deter you. If you want a driver's license, will you change your mind about that simply because you fail your test on the first attempt? Go for it again and again. It is never over until you achieve it. You are an achiever. God says you are, and by faith you can do it.

PATIENCE OF FAITH

For ye have need of patience, that, after ye have done the will of God, ye might receive the promise. For yet a little while, and He that shall come will come, and will not tarry (Hebrews 10:36-37).

There is always a little while between the time you release your faith and the time of manifestation. A lot of things might happen in the period between, and if you are not patient, you will destroy what is in the pipeline. Patience is the capacity to tolerate delay, trouble, or suffering without becoming angry or upset while you are waiting for the fulfillment of the promise. You need to be patient, because your miracle, your expectation, or your breakthrough can only come in a particular season and in God's own appointed time.

For the vision is yet for an appointed time, but at the end it shall speak, and not lie: though it tarry, wait for it; because it will surely come, it will not tarry (Habakkuk 2:3).

There is a season of harvest, a season of promotion, and a season of favor. Your breakthrough has a season. Whatever God will do for you will come in its season; you must be patient. Patience involves waiting, and waiting has to do with expectancy. As you wait, keep expecting it to happen. In waiting, you need to learn to be quiet. "It is good that a man should both hope and quietly wait for the salvation of the Lord" (Lam. 3:26). Quietness here means the absence of fear, worry, or anxiety. Through patience, you can wait in quietness. It was 25 years from the time God promised Abraham a son until the time Isaac was born. It took Israel 685 years to get into the Promised Land from the time of promise to Abraham, through Jacob's journey into Egypt, right up to the time of Moses and the entrance into Canaan. It took David about 18 years to become king in Israel after he was anointed by the prophet Samuel.

ENDURANCE OF FAITH

Endurance is the ability to go through hardship without giving up or surrendering to defeat. Endurance helps you contain the hardship you encounter on your way to destiny. It helps you suffer until what you are suffering for happens. Faith does not perform miracles in all seasons. What do I mean? God does everything in its season, so the thing that your faith is released for can only come in the season God has set. But whatever the season, faith says that the thing has already been done. Faith gives you the assurance that what you hope for is done.

Faith produces endurance because discouraging things might happen, there might be hardship on the way, and there may be a long period of waiting. There can be suffering in waiting, as the Bible says, *"Hope deferred maketh the heart sick..."* (Prov. 13:12). But because faith says that what you hope for is done, it gives you the ability to tolerate hardship and the courage and strength to hold on and wait for the manifestation. Faith releases the ability to endure hardship.

TEMPERANCE OF FAITH

Temperance is the ability to restrain yourself from something you should not do but may want to do. I have said that between the place of faith and the fulfillment of promise there might be troubles, crises, hardship, and difficulties. It is possible at this stage to have a change of vision, and it is possible to also change the direction you are going. What will keep you on track is your ability to be temperate.

Inconsistency will not prosper anybody. If you believe that what you are holding on to God for has not eluded you and will surely come through, then stay where you are.

JOY OF FAITH

Faith releases joy in your spirit. The very fact that you know that you are a child of destiny and your future is secured gives you joy. Joy is different from happiness. Happiness is based on the senses—it is the feeling of pleasure because of what has happened to you. Joy springs from your spirit—it does not come as a result of what you see or hear. It is a faith thing; it is an anointing.

> *Then he said unto them, Go your way, eat the fat, and drink the sweet, and send portions unto them for whom nothing is prepared: for this day is holy unto our Lord: neither be ye sorry; for the joy of the Lord is your strength* (Nehemiah 8:10).

Joy is strength. It was joy that empowered Jesus to go through Calvary (see Heb. 12:2). It is the joy of becoming a mother that helps a woman through nine months of pregnancy and the process of child labor. After she has one child, she wants another; joy makes her ignore the pain of delivery. If faith rises in your spirit, it releases joy so that you stand every trial of life with pleasure and watch to see your destiny established. Joy gives purpose and pleasure in living; it helps you not to feel dejected and rejected. It helps you find contentment in the midst of despair and look to the future with excitement because you know it will be all right.

MAKE GOD'S PROMISES HAPPEN

Know that God has the integrity and the capacity to make good His Word. A promise is only as good as the integrity of the person making the promise and his ability to make good his promises. When a man is not known for keeping his word—if he is known to be un-reliable—it will be hard to trust him. But not so with our God! He is trustworthy. He only says what He means, and He means whatever He says (see Num. 23:19).

Also, if a man does not have the capacity to make good his promises, even though he may have good intentions and be a reliable person, the fact that he doesn't fulfill his promises means that his promise is only a wish. You see, we can trust our God because He is not only faithful to His Word, He also has the capacity to make His promises happen. There is nothing that God cannot do, and there is nothing that He has promised that He will not deliver.

> *Ah Lord God! Behold, Thou hast made the Heaven and the earth by Thy great power and stretched out arm, and there is nothing too hard for Thee* (Jeremiah 32:17).

So no matter your situation—no matter how bad it has become, no matter what people are saying, no matter what your doctors say—just know that He is faithful and is able to do whatever He says. You've got to believe it and act like you know it is so. No one else's words will count if what they are saying is not what God is saying.

Continue to hold on to the word that you have received. Once the word is released, it is like a seed planted—it takes only a matter of time and it will come to pass if we hold on to it. To hold on to the word means to continue to believe that what He has promised is so, even when it appears that nothing is happening to our present condition. By this I mean that you remain unwavering, dogged in your conviction regarding His promises, even in the face of contradiction. In other words, nothing will make you change your mind about what you believe God for. It means to continue to confess and to declare that it is so and that it will come to pass, even when it makes you look stupid. It also means to continue to expect it to happen, even when it has gone past the time or season you initially expected.

You see, it is never too late with God—He always comes through. If you won't draw back but continue to hold on, even when it seems like it is never going to happen, He will come through for you. God's Word never returns to Him void; He does whatever He says. Hold on to the Word of God—keep seeing yourself in the light of it, keep believing it—and God will do it for you.

Walk in the fear of God. To have the fear of God simply means to live in a way that glorifies God.

> *He that walketh in his uprightness feareth the Lord: but he that is perverse in his ways despiseth Him* (Proverbs 14:2).

If you are holding on to God for something He has promised in His Word yet you are not living right and are not showing regard for Him in your lifestyle, how can you expect Him to have any regard for you? Some believers think that they can ignore God in their affairs, live a lifestyle of ungodliness, and God will still take charge of their affairs, hear their prayers, and make His Word fruitful in them, even though they have shown no regard for that Word. Some people treat God like men of God are more anointed than God Himself. They think they can have their breakthrough and achieve greatness irrespective of how they live when men of God lay hands on them and anoint them with oil. It is the fear of God that releases the blessing.

> *Blessed is every one that feareth the Lord; that walketh in His ways. For thou shalt eat the labor of thine hands: happy shalt thou be, and it shall be well with thee. Thy wife shall be as a fruitful vine by the sides of thine house: thy children like olive plants round about thy table. Behold, that thus shall the man be blessed that feareth the Lord* (Psalm 128:1-4).

ATTRACTING HIS REWARD

Being of service to God attracts a reward. A lot of times, answers to prayer also come as a reward for service. Remember when Hezekiah fell ill and the prophet told him to put his house in order because he was going to die? He did not just plead for the mercy of God, he referred God to his service to God in his prayer for healing, and God added fifteen more years to him (see 2 Kings 20:1-6).

When you are involved in the things of God and are serving Him fruitfully, He will answer your prayer and will meet your needs. The Bible says:

You did not choose Me, but I chose you and appointed you to go and bear fruit—fruit that will last. Then the Father will give you whatever you ask in My name (John 15:16 NIV).

He is a faithful God. No matter how busy you get, as a believer you must create time to serve and be faithful and selfless. Do not make yourself unprofitable. Never expect the Kingdom to pay attention to you when you don't care about the affairs of the Kingdom. It is the law of harvest. When you serve God, He says He will not be unrighteous to forget you. He says:

And ye shall serve the Lord your God, and He shall bless thy bread, and thy water; and I will take sickness away from the midst of thee. There shall nothing cast their young, nor be barren, in thy land: the number of thy days I will fulfill (Exodus 23:25-26).

FULFILLING THE CONDITION

It is important to remember that some promises and prophecies of God come with conditions. Sometimes God requires that you do something, act in a particular way, or sow a particular seed to release the anointing in the Word before it can happen. Don't just do nothing and expect it to happen. It is important that you understand the prophecies spoken into your life.

Learn to always listen to what the promise or prophecy says you must do to make it happen. If you set aside what it says to do, nothing is going to happen. If you are walking in the light of what the Word says, it is only a matter of time—it will happen to you. It may tarry, but it will surely come to pass. God never says something that He can't bring about.

As stated earlier, some prophecies or promises do not happen automatically because of the law of harvest. The law of harvest is an eternal principle of life—it determines destinies. Your life is the product of harvest; your harvest is the outcome of the seed you have sown in the past. Where you will go in the future and what you will have or become in life will be determined by the seeds you are sowing. The law of harvest also applies to how we relate with God. If you are not faithful to Him, how can you expect to profit from His faithfulness? God is not mocked. If you are never faithful to Him, then know that you do not have the right to lay claim to His promises (see 1 Sam. 2:30).

You honor God by giving Him His due place in your life, recognizing Him in all your affairs, obeying His Word, and doing what He says. You also honor God when you demonstrate that you love Him most of all.

SIX WAYS TO HONOR GOD

1. God is honored when you don't put your substance into anything that dishonors God or promotes unrighteousness.

   A believer should not use his money to facilitate anything that is anti-God. For instance, a child of God must not use his money to build the synagogue of satan or invest in ventures that advance evil and promote ungodliness like pubs and bars, paying for sex, pornographic materials, et cetera. Look closely into what you are investing into and what you are spending your money on.

2. God is honored when you use your substance for His purposes.

   Use your money to feed the hungry, sponsor orphans, feed widows, help to sponsor church plants and the spread of the Gospel, help to pay for the welfare of missionaries, and improve somebody's life. When you use what you have to be a blessing, God is honored.

3. When you give an offering of thanksgiving.

    God wants you to take out an offering from what you have and give to Him when you appear before Him. He is honored when we give to Him for thanksgiving from our storehouse or accounts. When you take from what you have and give to God for thanksgiving, you show that whatever you have achieved, acquired, or become has come about by His power.

    It is also important for you to know that when you come to give an offering of thanksgiving, you do not present to God what is not of value to you—a leftover that you would not give to a human being that you have regard for. It must be substantial; essentially, it must be something which has meaning to you.

4. Honoring God with your tithes.

    The tithe is the tenth of all income. I know a lot of believers are familiar with tithes, but how many are faithful to God with their tithes? God says we are robbing Him of what belongs to Him when we do not give Him the tithes and the offerings (see Mal. 3:8-12).

5. Obedience with the firstfruits of your increase.

    A lot of believers do not realize that everything from the womb of man or beast and the first harvest of the field are to be dedicated unto God—they are to be treated as belonging to God. The Scripture specifically says, "Honor the Lord with thy substance, and with the firstfruits of all thine increase" (Prov. 3:9).

    It is important that you know that the first of every increase belongs to God—the first salary in a new job, the first portion of the first increment in a salary, the first profit or dividend in every investment, et cetera.

    Thou shalt not delay to offer the first of thy ripe fruits, and of thy liquors: the firstborn of thy sons shalt thou give unto

Me. Likewise shalt thou do with thine oxen, and with thy
sheep: seven days it shall be with his dam; on the eighth
day thou shalt give it Me (Exodus 22:29-30).

6.   Honoring the man of God.

A lot of believers do not realize that no matter how highly
anointed a man of God is there is a limit to which his
anointing can benefit you. If he is being a blessing to you in
the ministry of the Word and you are not ministering back
to him in material things, then you will not be benefiting
at the level which you could be. The way the Kingdom of
God operates is a believer who is taught the Word of God
should minister back to the person who teaches him the
Word of God in every good thing of life.

Let him that is taught in the word communicate unto him
that teacheth in all good things. Be not deceived; God is
not mocked; for whatsoever a man soweth, that shall he
also reap (Galatians 6:6-7).

Anytime you receive a word and you believe it is inspired
for you, key in to it by sowing a seed to allow the grace on
the man's life to work for you. It is important that, from
time to time, you take out something from your increase
to minister back to the person that God has put in your life
to minister to you in spiritual things. There is a difference
between just being a generous giver—having the heart
of giving to meet needs in people's lives—and giving to
a man of God simply because of his ministry to you and
because you can see the hand of God on his life.

A good example here is the story of the prophet and the
Shunamite woman (see 2 Kings 4:8-17). The Shunamite
woman was a natural giver and was very hospitable to the
prophet many times. She saw the grace of God in his life
and she ministered to him; that attracted the blessing.

If you look closely in every church, you will see that the
people who are being blessed most through the ministry

of the pastor are those who are ministering back to him in earthly things. It is the law of harvest. If a man is truly called of God to be a minister, then there is an anointing in his life to help others develop spiritually, inspire them to dream, and empower them to achieve their purpose. Every man of God has the grace of God to impact the people he has been assigned to. His ministry can heal them and transform their entire life. But there is a limit to how much impact his anointing can have if you are not sowing back into his life. That is how it works; it is the law of harvest.

Chapter Three

Experiencing God's Increase

Though thy beginning was small, yet thy latter end should greatly increase (Job 8:7).

I believe that everybody reading this book would like to experience increase in his or her life or move to a higher level in something. It may be in your career, marriage, finances, or spirituality. Nobody really appreciates stagnation or retrogression. We all want to see increase in all spheres of our lives. Increase does not happen to anybody accidentally—people have to do something to make it happen. No one who has accomplished something in life ever just wakes up one day to discover that a big change happened to them overnight—they all do something to make that change happen. We have all got to do something to attract God's increase in our lives. I want to share five principles of increase here, and I believe that if you walk in the light of them, they will pave the way for you to move to a higher level in life and experience the increase that you would love to have.

THE RIGHT MINDSET

There are three things I would like you to grasp here. First, you need to walk conscious of the fact that God is a God of increase. He is the One who brings the increase.

I have planted, Apollos watered; but God gave the increase (1 Corinthians 3:6).

Second, you need to believe that it is God's will for you to have increase. You must know that God is never going to be glorified through your failure—only the devil is glorified when we fail. Believe it—God delights in your prosperity; He wants you to increase and enlarge.

Though thy beginning was small, yet thy latter end should greatly increase (Job 8:7).

Third, God will only give increase in order to make you a blessing, not for your pride in it or for your lustful consumption. Increase comes for the majesty and increase of His Kingdom. God won't bring increase into your life if it will compete with Him and become a god to you.

OBEY THE LEADING OF GOD

Thus saith the Lord, thy Redeemer, the Holy One of Israel: I am the Lord thy God which teacheth thee to profit, which lead-eth thee by the way that thou shouldest go (Isaiah 48:17).

God is going to show you how to walk in increase, and He will lead you in that walk. Sometimes He will ask you to do things that might appear stupid or unreasonable to you. However, you must know that increase is tied to your obedience to what He says, even if what He says does not make any sense to you. An example of this is when God asked Abraham to sacrifice Isaac. Do not be afraid to follow the leading of God for your life, because He has got your best interests at heart and will never lead you to do anything that will destroy you.

For I know the thoughts that I think toward you, saith the Lord, thoughts of peace, and not of evil, to give you an expected end (Jeremiah 29:11).

DETERMINE TO ACHIEVE YOUR GOAL

Have a dream and create its picture in your mind. Let it be your passion and motivation, and let it be what you are living for. You have set a goal for yourself, and as long as you have not reached that goal you will always know that God is not through with you, and you will not be satisfied until you reach it.

You will need a bit of determination, because you are not going to achieve your goal in one day. Between now and when you arrive at higher levels, things are sometimes going to appear tough and impossible. The devil is not going to lose sleep over what you are trusting the Lord for. He will try to resist every effort you make; he will try to make things appear as though you are not really making any meaningful progress; he will give you a picture of defeat; and he will seek to frustrate you. But no matter what happens, maintain your confidence in the Lord and set your focus on the things you believe to be God's destiny for you. Do not allow satan to make you accept the present—this is not where you belong; it is going to pass. Look through history and you will see that the people who have achieved something meaningful and impacted their generation were those who showed courage and determination and were persistent in the face of all odds. Whatever you can see, you can become.

MAKE YOURSELF MARKETABLE

If you want to make yourself valuable to people, you need to exhibit the following virtues in your work and in your dealings with people: hard work, integrity, and faithfulness in everything.

To me, hard work means to stop complaining about your job. Stop undermining what God has given to you now. Get into it and give it your best shot. The Bible says, "Whatsoever thy hand findeth to do, do it with thy might..." (Eccles. 9:10).

In doing your job, learn to do the extras—volunteer to do for free the jobs that your colleagues will not. Do those jobs well, without asking to be paid for them. Learn to stay at your work place beyond your contracted hours if need be without asking to be paid for it. Learn to assist your colleagues in their jobs, and learn to do what you know is right to do without being told. Be self-instructive.

Integrity is about being honest, reliable, and consistent. Your integrity will make you valuable to people, because it gives you a good name and a good name attracts favor. The Bible says, "A good name is rather to be chosen than great riches, and loving favor rather than silver and gold" (Prov. 22:1).

The Bible also says a good name is more attractive than the most expensive perfume (see Eccles. 7:1). Integrity makes people want to trust you, depend on you, and introduce you. It helps you develop depth with people that God has connected you to. Integrity will open you to people of calibers you never thought you could associate with. Being a man or woman of integrity means that you are a person:

- Whose character reflects good behavior both in the sight of God and man. You must be somebody who deals with people in good conscience. Don't use people, don't take advantage of them, and don't take them for granted.

- Who will not be yoked with men and women of dubious character. Your association defines you. It is said, "Show me your friends, and I will tell you who you are." Your association says a lot about you.

- Who makes promises or pledges and keeps them. Your word must be your bond; you must be trusted. If you cannot be trusted with your words, you have a big problem.

- Who will return money when you have been overpaid.

- Who will keep detailed records of expenses, especially when acting in a transaction on behalf of somebody.

- Who will avoid buying anything on credit, especially if you are not sure that you will be able to pay it back on the due date.

- Who will pay your bills promptly. No lender will want to give anybody money when he is defaulting in payments. Defaults in payments affect your credit worthiness.

- Who will not defraud the government of taxes.

- Who will not want to make money in a dubious manner.

- Who will not falsify documents.

Do you realize that one of God's criteria for increase is faithfulness? God does not start with anyone at the peak of His purpose for that person. Normally, He determines a person's destiny but starts with him at the base and leads him from one level to the next until he arrives at his destiny. The period between the base and the destiny is training and testing time. If God can find you faithful at each level, He lifts you up to the next level. If He can trust you with a cleaning job, He can trust you with a managerial job. If He can trust you with fifty congregation members, He can trust you with a hundred.

> *Whoever can be trusted with very little can also be trusted with much, and whoever is dishonest with very little will also be dishonest with much. So if you have not been trustworthy in handling worldly wealth, who will trust you with true riches? And if you have not been trustworthy with someone else's property, who will give you property of your own?* (Luke 16:10-12 NIV)

One of the reasons God requires us to be faithful in everything He has put under our care is because we are *His* stewards (see 1 Cor. 4:1-2). A steward is someone who takes care of another person's property on their behalf. Everything that you are today and will be in the future and everything you have now and will have in the future will come through God. He owns everything (see Ps. 24:1).

You must start to see anything good that happens to you as coming from God on the grounds of stewardship. It really does not matter who your employer is or what job you are doing right now—just see God as your employer. Do your work as if you are serving Christ. See yourself as His steward wherever you are and in whatever you find yourself doing.

Servants, obey in all things your masters according to the flesh; not with eyeservice, as menpleasers; but in singleness of heart, fearing God; and whatsoever ye do, do it heartily, as to the Lord, and not unto men; knowing that of the Lord ye shall receive the reward of the inheritance: for ye serve the Lord Christ (Colossians 3:22-24).

Doing your work as unto God means to do your work with dedication, working in the fear of God—the first priority being the glory of God, not material benefit. A good steward does not work for his own interest first but for the interest of the owner. He does not seek after his own profit but the profit of him whom he serves.

It also means to work with cheerfulness. You need to find joy in your job, no matter what level you are at right now. If you can find joy, that joy will be your strength. If you enjoy your work, you will not go to work late or take advantage of your quiet colleagues and leave them to do all the work. You will not be inclined to call off sick when you don't have to, and you will not be given to instability, running from one job to the other.

BE INVESTMENT-ORIENTED

When God gives you something, He wants you to see it as a seed first and not as bread. Not everything that you get is meant for the belly—you must learn to separate the gift for the belly and the one for seed.

Now he that ministereth seed to the sower both minister bread for your food, and multiply your seed sown, and increase the fruits of your righteousness; being enriched in every thing to all bountifulness, which causeth through us thanksgiving to God (2 Corinthians 9:10-11).

The potential for increase is inside of everything that God blesses you with, but you must start to see that you are blessed with seeds first and not bread. The law of harvest says you will reap what you sow. You have got to sow your seed to get a harvest. There are many ways you can invest what you have as seed. When what you have cannot meet your immediate need, look for the person whose need it can meet and be a blessing to him.

Always look for ways you can use your resources for the work of the ministry. This is not only about your tithes and offerings—sow into missionary ventures and the lives of men of God, especially those that minister to you directly in spiritual things. Learn to look out for the poor and make yourself a blessing to them. You can also give to the poor by financing the work of charities like African missions run by RCCG, Christian Aid, Open Kingdom, and so on (you can find these charities online). One other way to sow is by the seed of faith. The seed of faith is when you are giving to God to believe Him for something. Believe me, there is power in sowing seed. Seeds and vows do the same thing. With them we show our helplessness and our faith in God.

Please know that you cannot bribe God, you cannot buy the grace of God, and you cannot pay for any of God's goodness. Your seed only shows that you are helpless and are relying on God for your expectations to happen. Nothing may happen the first time you sow seed toward a thing, and it is possible that nothing will happen the second and the third time. But someday your seed will come before God for a memorial and it will speak for you. Make seed-sowing a lifestyle, and anytime there is a chance to sow a seed, please do so. Do not just give without a purpose, especially if you are believing God for something. Use your seed to remind God of your desire.

Chapter Four

Breaking the Yoke of Bondage

Stand fast therefore in the liberty wherewith Christ hath made us free, and be not entangled again with the yoke of bondage. ...For, brethren, ye have been called unto liberty; only use not liberty for an occasion to the flesh, but by love serve one another (Galatians 5:1,13).

It is of utmost importance as a believer that you know you are free from bondage, you keep your freedom, and you go about your life aware of your freedom in Christ Jesus. The Bible says that Christ has set us free, so it is not God's will that we walk in bondage. We were made totally free when we invited Jesus into our lives and were born again. You must allow that to settle in your spirit. Bondage is when someone is under domination, has lost his right of self-determination, or is under oppression. When someone is in bondage, his power of self-determination is being usurped and controlled. The person is sometimes compelled to do things that he would not ordinarily do. Satan is the one who puts people in bondage. He wants people in bondage because he knows that if he can get somebody bound he will be able to hinder God from fulfilling His purpose in that person's life.

Satan knows that until we are completely free God cannot lead us and will not be able to fulfill His plans for our lives. That is why the devil (in the form of Pharaoh) would not let Israel leave Egypt—he knew God had a plan for them. He knew that the seed of the woman would come from them and the nations would be redeemed. He knew he would be able to hinder that divine plan if he could keep Israel in bonds. In bondage, you cannot fulfill your purpose. There are different mediums that the devil uses to subject people to bondage. I want to share some with you so that you can keep vigil over your life and not give satan that chance.

THE BONDAGE OF HUMAN CONTROL

Human control falls under the spirit of witchcraft. You do not have to cast spells on people or put a curse on someone to be a witch. Anything that tries to replace God's influence over people is witchcraft. So, a person practices witchcraft any time he tries to replace God in people's lives, and you are under the influence of witchcraft anytime you allow people to replace God in your life. Witchcraft expresses itself in four ways—manipulation, domination, intimidation, and control.

Manipulation happens when somebody is using schemes to get people to do what they would ordinarily not do, left to their own discretion or judgment and their own power of choice. Domination is when someone is being suppressed by another person. When someone is dominated, the person who dominates him controls his will and determines what the person does, who he sees, what he eats or wears, and all that. The dominant person always thinks he knows better regarding what is good for the person and has the right to decide for him.

Domination is empowered by fear and dependence. The dominant person uses fear and guilt to suppress and control his victim. For example, a woman can easily be a victim of control when she stays with a man simply because she is afraid of the stigma of divorce, is afraid of being single, or is afraid that she may never find somebody as good as him. I am not advocating divorce here at all, but nobody should stay in a relationship because of fear—fear is oppressive. When you show to someone that you cannot do without him, he will want to control your life. Any relationship that is based on control and not respect and love will not bring prosperity and true happiness. There is a difference between the authority that God bestowed upon a husband over his wife in a marriage relationship and domination, which is witchcraft. It is witchcraft to play God in somebody's life.

Intimidation happens when somebody is using threats, terror, reactions, mood, and attitude to get you to change your opinion and do what they want, not what you want to do. Sometimes actions like the use of tears, pleading, and gifts or favor can be controlling, too. To overcome this sort of witchcraft, you must know what you really want for yourself. You need to know God's will for you and stick to it. If you do not know what you really want and what God is doing in you, somebody around you who is controlling is going to make you do what he or she wants.

Controlling spirits, in the church especially, like to imitate God. They can sometimes speak as if in prophecy because they know that you love the Lord and will want to obey Him. Do not marry anybody or go into business with anybody simply because he says, "Thus says the Lord." You must learn to know the plan of God for your life by yourself.

You need boldness to overcome intimidation and control. It takes boldness to be able to say "no" and not feel guilty when you really need to say it. People who do not know how to say no can easily become victims. Be nice, but do not let people's feelings, attitudes, or reactions impair your judgment. This means overcoming the fear of man and dependence on man. Learn to put your trust in no man, only in the Lord. Do not live under the fear that somebody might abandon you and ruin your whole life. Nobody can determine your destiny—only God does. You will be OK as long as God is not leaving you.

BONDAGE THROUGH DEMONIC CONTROL

There are millions and millions of demons out there that have been unleashed by satan to interrupt God's plan and enthrone satan in the hearts and affairs of men. These demons seek to infiltrate every segment of our society and pollute it. They seek to control our minds so that we lose our sense of godliness and live like we have no regard for God. They distort our sense of morality by their influence in our life-styles, afflict our families, and disrupt the plans of God for humanity.

These demons are in different categories, and each category is responsible for a particular kind of behavioral disorder. For example, there is a demon responsible for immorality, there is a demon behind fear, and there are demons responsible for drunkenness, violence, murder, suicide, et cetera. The kind of demon that controls a man can be known by what he acts out. You can tell what spirit is in a man by his behavior or lifestyle.

Demons seek to gain control in a subtle manner, using enticement and seduction to trap their victim. They employ the senses to get their victim obsessed with a thing, intending to use that thing to bring him under their influence. What you see, hear, touch, taste, and smell can be the gateway that can open up your life to the devil. It is important to note that demons do not seek to gain control over a person just for the sake of it. Their intention is always to damage you. For instance, if demons are able to bring you into bondage to drugs, nicotine, or alcohol, they will eventually use that to damage your health, rob you of your job and finances, and break and destroy every relationship that you have. If they can get you to be a slave to sexual immorality and perversion, they will want to use that to steal your finances, break and destroy your relationships, put you into problems with the law, bring you into shame, and even afflict you with disease.

Unforgiveness, bitterness, misery, and misfortune are also avenues that demons use to access people. They cause depression and sicknesses. There is a demon behind depression; if he can lock himself in you, he will make you believe that you are no good, that God is against you, that the world is against you, and that life is not worth living. He will make you feel unwanted and not useful and will cut you off from people who really care about you. His ultimate goal is to make you consider suicide. Please ask your pastor to pray with you if you are feeling this way.

The experience of misfortune, loss, and the sense of failure are also occasions that depression looks for. No matter what, do not let the devil steal your joy. Do not let what you are experiencing make you think less of yourself. The fact that you are going through that hardship or challenge does not mean that you are rejected—God is not through with you yet.

Social violence is a spirit. It does not take root and express itself in one day; it develops over time. A lot of times it stems out of unforgiveness, fear, inferiority complexes, and lack of contentment. Most people who are being used by this demon to control people were themselves victims of social injustice or abuse at one point in their lives. To keep clear of demons, you must stay clear of anything satanic—Tarot cards, palm reading, and all forms of sexual perversions and immoralities. Do not harbor hurts or unforgiveness. Stay clear of bitterness because it is a gateway. Learn to forgive whatever wrong is done against you. Should you start to see yourself drifting and starting to entertain such things, go to God and ask Him to help you and seek counsel.

BONDAGE THROUGH RELIGION

Religion is one of the powerful weapons that satan uses to keep people bound. Christianity is more than religion—it is about relationship with God through Jesus. It is a lifestyle that reflects God and His goodness. Religion replaces faith with good works. In religion, good works make you feel good and accepted by God. In religion, you think you can attain higher spirituality through good works and the Lord will bless you on that basis. But in reality, our good works are like filthy rags before God, and no one can be righteous or acceptable to God by works (see Isa. 64:6). Does that mean that in Christ good works do not count? No—through our works we demonstrate our faith, show that we are saved, and demonstrate our appreciation of His salvation. Our works do not earn us salvation—they show that God works through us.

Religion focuses more on rules, regulations, and duties than on relationship with God. The difference between Jesus and the Pharisees was the fact that they were more particular about rules and rituals, whereas Jesus taught about the relationship between God and man. Religious people may adhere to religious rules without necessarily trusting God with their lives. A good example of this is the case of the young rich ruler (see Mark 10:17,21-22). He tried to observe all the laws of Moses but did not trust God with his life.

Christianity is not religion—it is a relationship with God through Jesus Christ based on faith. You cannot claim to have faith in God if you cannot allow Him to have control of your life and all you have. You can keep all the rules, but it is only going to amount to religion if Christ is not Lord in your life. You must trust Him with your life, marriage, career, and wealth. Are there rules and regulations in Christianity, and do we have boundaries? Yes, there are rules and boundaries, but they are not what make us saved. The rules are there to guide us in our relationship with God and with one another. We are not to put more attention on religious rituals, man-made church doctrines, and traditions than on relationship with God.

Religion makes an outward show of holiness and humility. Religious people like to portray godliness and show that they are intimate with God, but their humility is false—they are hypocrites. What they portray is what they want people to think of them, because they like the praise of men more than God's approval. On the inside they are full of pride, jealousy, hatred, murder, lust, and greed (see Matt. 23:25-28).

Religious people are "churchy." There is nothing wrong with loving church and going to church faithfully. As far as I can remember, I have never stayed home on a Sunday since I gave my life to Jesus, except when ill, and I hardly fall ill—I enjoy divine health. I love to be in church, not because I am "churchy," but because I get nourished there and I like to spend time with the brethren. However, going to church can become just another religious practice when going to church, Bible study, and prayer meetings becomes a religious obligation or when your church activities become mere rituals. Ritual is when your Christianity has no life and is not a witness to the world around you. When your life is not being a blessing to somebody, despite your church attendance, you are just a church man or woman and it is just religion you are playing. That is the point the devil would love to bring everybody to.

The devil is not bothered with your church attendance, your tithing, or any of the other Christian activities that you are involved with as long as your life is not being transformed by the Word of God and you are not being the witness to the world that God intends you to be. What do you go to church to see? What contributions do you make? In what way is it challenging and helping to shape your life?

Religious people are more particular about church denomination. A religious man will have this thing about his own church denomination and will feel that what his church believes in is the best. Anywhere he goes, he will only want to be part of his denomination, and if it is not there he will feel that there are no good churches around. In Christ Jesus, what is important is faith which works through love (see Gal. 5:6). I believe that it is not of God to think that one denomination is the best, its teachings are absolute, and people who are not part of it are not genuinely saved and will not make it to Heaven. God is bigger than a little denomination; the Church of God is definitely beyond any little group. We must start to see God in other churches and appreciate Him for what He is doing. We must be willing to be involved with any church if God calls us there.

BONDAGE THROUGH
MATERIALISTIC CONTROL

Materialistic bondage is another form of idolatry. It can be identified in three forms—unhealthy desire or craving for material things, ungodly desperation in pursuit of material things, and ungodly attachment to material possessions. All these are materialism. If you are somebody who easily gets attached to possessions and will not easily let go, there are certain blessings that God will not bless you with.

There are two reasons God will not bless you with some things if you are attached to them. First, it is because God is a jealous God and will not want to compete with anything in your life (see Exod. 20:5). Second, we are God's stewards and are meant to be channels of blessings. Whatever God gives is meant to be used for His glory and shared. God can bless you freely only when He knows that He can get it back anytime He needs it. There are several things needed to overcome material bondage.

- You must learn not to be attached to whatever God has blessed you with, and you must be willing to let go any time and any day the Lord places a demand on it.

- Know that whatever is meant to be yours the Lord will replace even more when you give it away. If you give away something that is meant to be yours because God says to do so, it is only going to be a seed.

- Know that anytime God wants to bring increase into your life, He demands seed.

You must overcome the fear of losing what you have. If you do not, you may want to use any means to keep it, and that will destroy you (see 1 Kings 11:29-32; 12:20,26-30). You also need to always remember that whatever did not come to you by your power can only be sustained by the power that made it possible for you to have it.

If God will not give you something, do not try to have it by any means. If you do, it will become a snare (see 1 Kings 21:1-16; 2 Kings 5:15-27). Do not wish to have what everybody is having and do not wish to become what everybody is going for. If you do, you might end up doing what everybody is doing to get it, even if what they are doing does not glorify God. Just desire to be what God has called you to be.

Chapter Five

Out of Darkness Into His Marvelous Light

But ye are a chosen generation, a royal priesthood, an holy nation, a peculiar people; that ye should shew forth the praises of Him who hath called you out of darkness into His marvelous light (1 Peter 2:9).

There are four things God has made us, as we can see from the above passage. Remember, the Bible did not say we will become this—it says that we are. *God* is saying we are a chosen generation, a royal priesthood, a holy nation, and a peculiar people. He made us that so we can show forth His glorious light. We cannot show forth His light until we know that we are really what He says we are, start to believe it, see ourselves as that, and start to behave like we know who we really are. Now let us look at each more closely.

THE CHOSEN GENERATION

It is important to remind ourselves of the truth that nobody gets saved simply because he decided to. We know that we are saved because the Lord Himself decreed our salvation long before we were born, as the Scriptures have showed us (see Eph. 1:3-5). For example, God said to Jeremiah:

Before I formed thee in the belly I knew thee; and before thou camest forth out of the womb I sanctified thee, and I ordained thee a prophet unto the nations (Jeremiah 1:5).

The Lord also said concerning Esau and Jacob while they were in the womb:

As it is written, Jacob have I loved, but Esau have I hated. What then shall we say? Is there unrighteousness with God? God forbid. ...So then it is neither of him that willeth, nor of him that runneth, but of God that showeth mercy (Romans 9:13-14,16).

Your salvation is by election; God elected you to be free from bondage and live life in abundance. You did not vote for Him—He elected you, and He did that a long time ago, even before you were conceived. Why do we preach, if salvation is by God's election? We preach to bring into the fold God's elects. It is the preaching of the Gospel that fishes out the elect. When the elect hear the Word, the seed of faith is released in them by the Holy Spirit, so they are able to understand the Word, believe it, and receive it. Nobody can believe the Gospel by himself—it is the working of the grace of God.

That in the ages to come He might shew the exceeding riches of His grace in His kindness toward us through Christ Jesus. For by grace are ye saved through faith; and that not of yourselves: it is the gift of God: not of works, lest any man should boast (Ephesians 2:7-9).

It is important to realize that everything God does is for a purpose. God chose us in Christ for a purpose. Paul admonishes that we should pray so that we can understand the purpose of our calling (see Eph. 1:15-18). We all know that God wants us to be healthy people, not sickly. We know that He wants us to be prosperous people and not poor people, successful people and not failures. We know He wants us to be free from any form of oppression or bondage. These are precious and wonderful privileges and we do need them, however, they are not God's ultimate plan for us. They are not the very reason why we were chosen by God.

Health, prosperity, and success are all the harvest, benefits, or products of the purpose for our election. They happen to us when we find our purpose in God and walk in the light of it. It is a misplacement of priority to pursue God's benefits first and not the very purpose for our calling. Today, people are invited to give their lives to Jesus so that they can start to walk in prosperity; I think this is a distortion of the Gospel. To only walk in prosperity is not the reason why He chose you.

THE GOD OF COVENANT

God is a covenant God. He chose you so you can enter into a covenant relationship with Him. Each person needs to understand the covenant you have with God through Jesus. A covenant is a solemn agreement that is made between two or more people with a promise to commit themselves to certain obligations. A covenant is not really a covenant until the parties concerned enter into it with an intention to make the terms of the covenant binding to them. Every covenant gives the parties in the covenant some rights and privileges. Most covenants are sealed with the shedding of blood or with the exchange of tokens.

When Jesus was offering His blood at Calvary, He was not only paying the penalty for sin and dying to save sinners, He was also initiating a new covenant with God on behalf of as many as will come to God through Him. His shed blood sprinkled on the mercy seat in the heavenly tabernacle was the token for the new covenant (see Heb. 9:11-12). This covenant is called the new covenant because there was a covenant that existed before—the covenant between God and Israel. The new covenant replaced that covenant. The new covenant is between God and as many as will come to Him through Jesus—the Church. The Church, the chosen or the called ones, has a covenant relationship with God through the death and the sacrifice of the blood of Jesus. We are the new covenant people, and our relationship with God under the new covenant is different from the relationship that God had with the people of Israel under the old covenant.

THE COVENANT

As said earlier, a covenant is a solemn agreement that is made between two or more people with a promise to commit themselves to certain obligations. This, I believe, is what the covenant we have with God looks like.

The Church's obligation in the covenant is that God will be the God of the Church. Your commitment to God must be that you are not going to allow anything else to become God in your life (see 2 Cor. 6:16).

The Church also commits to Jesus as the Lord and Savior of the Church. Your commitment must be that you are going to depend on Jesus for your entire life and not trust in your ability (see Eph. 5:23).

The Church will be separated from the world and be holy unto God. You are to commit to be different from the world and live a life that glorifies God (see 2 Cor. 6:17-18).

The Church will be an ecclesia—not only called out to be separated but called out to be ambassadors in the world. You are to be like light in darkness and the salt of the earth. You are to represent God wherever you are and speak for Him (see 2 Pet. 2:9).

The Church will be a pilgrim on the earth. You are to believe and to look forward to the coming of Jesus and the restoration of the Kingdom. You are not to live on earth like it is your final home but to set your affection on things above where Christ is seated (see 1 Pet. 2:11).

I believe that in the covenant God also committed Himself to several things. When God and Jesus were signing this covenant, they made several promises.

God will accept and not reject whosoever will come to God through Jesus, and anyone who comes to God through Jesus will receive forgiveness of sins (see John 6:37-38).

God will see and deal with whoever comes under the covenant as the righteousness of God (see 2 Cor. 5:21).

God will consider us not only as His covenant people, but will also consider us as sons (see Gal. 4:4-7).

We will be unto God a royal priesthood. This means that we will all have the right of access into His holy Presence. As such, we are all able to offer spiritual sacrifices acceptable to God (see 1 Pet. 2:9).

God will make us His holy habitation. This means that He will put His Spirit within us. We are now carriers of His holy Presence (see John 14:23).

THE FATHERHOOD OF GOD

The Fatherhood of God is one of God's primary intentions for our election. God is a Father and has always been. He wanted children, so He chose us so that we can be called the sons of God. If we are primarily called to be the sons of God, we need to make being sons of God our first priority in life. This will help us to strive to behave like the sons of God wherever we find ourselves. A child must have certain characteristics of the Father (see Eph. 5:1-2).

God has always wanted a family—a very large family. He called us so that we could be part of that large family (see Eph. 2:19-22). We need to start seeing ourselves as part of a large family, a family that is beyond our little sects or denominations. We need to start to see and treat every born-again person—white or brown, red or pink— as a brother or sister. Origin, background, and identity really do not matter—in Christ Jesus we are a family. Someday not very long from now, we are all going to be gathered together in one place called Heaven as one big family. God has always wanted that.

Having made known unto us the mystery of His will, according to His good pleasure which He hath purposed in Himself: that in the dispensation of the fullness of times He might gather together in one all things in Christ, both which are in Heaven, and which are on earth; even in Him (Ephesians 1:9-10).

HEIRS OF GOD

God did not call you to be His son or daughter only—He wants you to be His heir also (see Gal. 4:6-7). As God's heir, you have an eternal inheritance in God. You are entitled to receive and partake of the goodness of His Kingdom. And you are not meant to lack in any good thing which the Father wants to bless you with in life, because your Father God is a wealthy Father. He owns all the silver and the gold and the cattle on a thousand hills. Jesus actually died so that through His death there will be a legal ground for us to inherit God (see Heb. 9:15-17).

THE REVELATION OF HIS GLORY

God has always wanted the world to know His glory. He chose us so that the world, through us, may see His character, His beauty, and His goodness. We are to show forth His glory in the world. The world must see His divine wisdom and abilities through us.

> To the intent that now unto the principalities and powers in heavenly places might be known by the church the manifold wisdom of God, according to the eternal purpose which He purposed in Christ Jesus our Lord: in whom we have boldness and access with confidence by the faith of Him (Ephesians 3:10-12).

We must stand out in the crowd and be different. We must be the example of diligence, excellence, and hard work. We must be kind, compassionate, and forgiving, just as God is. We must not be lazy, immoral, and given to gluttony. We must stand out in the crowd as beacons of His glory. We are called to be different, and our difference will shine as light in the darkness of our world.

THE ROYAL PRIESTHOOD

We are a royal family because God our Father is the King of kings and the Lord of the earth. Actually, we are both kings and priests. In Christ, we have two identities. By virtue of our sonship to God, we have been made kings. We are also a kingdom of priests, because we belong to the family of Jesus the High Priest.

And hast made us unto our God kings and priests: and we shall reign on the earth (Revelation 5:10).

We need to understand that until we begin to function on the earth as kings and priests ordained by God, we may not experience the flow of His power in our lives or enter into the fullness of His blessings. Our ability to exercise our dominion over the earth is dependent on our understanding of our spiritual position with God.

As priests, we are primarily called to appear before God and to minister to people in the things pertaining to God. We are to offer to God worship and spiritual sacrifices.

Ye also, as lively stones, are built up a spiritual house, an holy priesthood, to offer up spiritual sacrifices, acceptable to God by Jesus Christ (1 Peter 2:5).

It is our duty as priests to give thanks to God on our behalf and on the behalf of others, irrespective of our circumstances. The Lord is worthy of our worship and praise no matter what. Until we learn to give Him the worship due to Him, we will not see the full manifestation of His power on the earth.

It is our duty as priests to stand in intercession before God on behalf of others.

For every high priest taken from among men is ordained for men in things pertaining to God, that he may offer both gifts and sacrifices for sins: who can have compassion on the ignorant, and on them that are out of the way; for that he himself also is compassed with infirmity. And by reason hereof he ought, as for the people, so also for himself, to offer for sins (Hebrews 5:1-3).

You must commit yourself to praying for your nation, city, and community. Pray for your colleagues who are not saved and pray for the brethren you know are going through challenges.

As priests, we are called to be teachers in things pertaining to God. In the Old Testament days, the priests were not only involved with rituals in the temple. They were also teachers of the law (see Ezra 7:6-10; Neh. 8:1-6).

> *And the things that thou hast heard of me among many witnesses, the same commit thou to faithful men, who shall be able to teach others also* (2 Timothy 2:2).

The Great Commission is a call for the Church to be teachers (see Matt. 28:19-20). It is the responsibility of the believer, every believer, to reach out and teach the world about Jesus. The early disciples of Jesus prioritized this, and they conquered the world of their time. We can, too, if we will only take our place and do what He commands us to do.

OUR FUNCTION AS KINGS

Kings sit on the throne and they rule. As kings, we are responsible for the physical affairs of people, and we are to exercise dominion on the earth for the benefit of people. In our functions as kings, we are to encourage and strengthen other people.

> *Let us therefore follow after the things which make for peace, and things wherewith one may edify another* (Romans 14:19).

It is out of order to be a discouragement to somebody or to constitute an obstacle to someone's success. Nobody must fail in life because of you, either by actions or by omissions.

We are kings to meet the needs of people both emotionally and materially. It does not matter what we think about ourselves—there is something that God has blessed us with so that we can be a blessing to somebody. Nobody called of God is empty. We are all blessed. Some of the things that we have without placing value on them are very much needed by somebody somewhere.

We are made kings so that we can help stop the work of the devil in the lives of people. We are to exercise control over sicknesses, poverty, and any form of the devil's oppression over people. On the Day of

Judgment, one of the things that the Lord will ask us will be regarding our involvement in the lives of people. Never ignore a chance to reach out and make a difference in somebody's life (see Matt. 25:34-40). Make every effort to invest into the lives of people; be the channel through which God can establish His purpose in the life of somebody.

THE PECULIAR PEOPLE

The word "peculiar" means unique, strange, or odd. God is saying here that we are a strange people—a new species of humans on the face of the earth. We are the wonder of Heaven, created in the Holy of Holies in Heaven where Jesus poured out His blood for our redemption. We are something new—a new type of people that the world has never seen before. We are called and chosen by God to be separated unto Him and be different from the people of the world. There should be something about us that uniquely distinguishes us from other people. For that to happen, we must first realize that we do not belong to this world (see John 15:19).

Since we are not of this world, we are the citizens of the Kingdom of Jesus—the citizens of Heaven. Since we do not belong to the world, we are expected by the Lord to be people with different values and different principles. The world system is not to determine our lifestyle. If you do not look strange or odd to the world, then you have completely missed the purpose of your calling, notwithstanding your commitment to a church. Wherever you go, people should take note of you, not because of the color of your skin or the clothes that you wear or the style of your hair, but for one thing—the impact Jesus has made in your life. There must be a difference between you and the people of the world. Several things make us peculiar.

Our Mentality

And do not be conformed to this world, but be transformed by the renewing of your mind, that you may prove what is that good and acceptable and perfect will of God (Romans 12:2 NKJV).

Now that we are born again, our way of thinking must change and be different from the way the world thinks. Our thinking should line up with the Word of God. We must not think the way the world thinks. We do not think too highly of ourselves. We do not think less of others or think evil of anybody. We do not consider success as about the name we make for ourselves but rather living our lives as He has called us to live.

Our mentality must be different from the people of the world. They think that the leaders are those that command people, but we think that the leader serves the people. The world thinks that you should do whatever makes you happy, but we allow the Word to constrain us—there are things we will not do because of our love for God. What they think is OK we know is not, because our line of thinking is being changed by His Word. The world thinks we are odd, foolish, religious, or from another planet, but we are only being what He has made us. We think differently.

Our Language

Wherefore, holy brethren, partakers of the heavenly calling, consider the Apostle and High Priest of our profession, Christ Jesus (Hebrews 3:1).

Whenever a Christian talks, what he says should line up with the Scriptures. Christianity is also called the great confession. You are to confess your faith, what you believe, and what the Word has said— not what you think, the situation, or what others have said. You must know that one of the priestly roles Jesus plays in the Holy of Holies in Heaven is the administration of our confession. What the Scripture above is saying is that Jesus is the High Priest of our confession. In Heaven, He administers your confession. You see, your confession determines how you are going to rise in life, so the Scripture adjourns to hold fast our profession or confession.

Seeing then that we have a great High Priest, that is passed into the heavens, Jesus the Son of God, let us hold fast our profession (Hebrews 4:14).

Jesus, as the High Priest of our confessions, takes what we say, puts it on the mercy seat, brings it under the blood of the covenant, and invokes the covenant. Therefore, through the workings of redemption and the priestly ministry of Jesus, our words become life and spirit. They justify us. Therefore, you must learn to operate through your words.

- Confess what the Word has said about who we are in Christ (see Col. 1:13-14).

- Confess that you are redeemed (see Col. 1:13-14).

- Confess that you are a new creation (see 2 Cor. 5:17)

- Confess that you are justified (see Rom. 4:25; 5:1).

- Confess that you are seated in the heavenly place in Christ far above all principalities (see Eph. 1:20-22; 2:6).

- Confess that you can do all things through Christ (see Phil. 4:13).

- Confess that you are redeemed from all curses (see Gal. 3:13).

- Confess that you are healed by His stripes (see 1 Pet. 2:24).

- Confess that you are blessed with all spiritual blessings in the heavenly places (see Eph. 1:3).

Your conversation should not just be about yourself—always be mindful that whatever you say is seasoned for the benefit of your hearers. In other words, what you say must be such that it brings enlightenment and encouragement to people (see Col. 4:6). People should be comforted by your words. Do not say, "I am just going to be blunt and straightforward about it. I will say it just as it is, and if they do not like it that is their problem." No, your words must not only be right, but considerate, kind, encouraging, enlightening, and empowering—seasoned with salt. Wherever you are, whatever you say should be for exhortation, edification, and the comfort of your hearers.

Your conversation must also show what sort of person you are. It must be a witness of your relationship with God. People should know that you are a child of God from your conversation. Whoever hears you talk should be able to tell that you are a child of God. That is why you are never to engage in any conversation to such an extent that you forget that you are a Christian. Your principle should be no guile, swearing, cursing, gossiping, or slandering of people (see Col. 3:8-9). You cannot talk like the world—you are a peculiar person. There are certain words that must never be heard from you.

Our Values

Our focus and emphasis in life must be different from the people of the world. The things of this world must not be more important to us than spiritual things or Heaven. People of this world live like the earth is their final destination; their emphasis is more on what they can have or become here and what they can achieve. That should not be the case for peculiar people. People of the world are only concerned about what gives them momentary happiness and pleasure—they are concerned about success, money, sex, fame, and power. But that should not be the case for us.

Our pursuits should be first to increase God's Kingdom and to see Him glorified in our lives and on the earth. Money, wealth, and fame have power over the people of the world—these things are their god—but to the new creation, whatever he becomes or possesses should be a tool to enrich and expand the Lord's Kingdom. The people of the world are worldly centered—they are afraid of dying—but the new creation, the peculiar people, should be Heaven-conscious and look with joy to our union with our Lord.

Our Behavior

The Word is our code of conduct, so our actions should always line up with the Word. The way we get involved with things, relate with people, and go about our affairs should be in line with the Word and in obedience to God. As people of the Kingdom of Heaven, we must not limit ourselves to what people think or say. Our upbringing, culture, traditions, or what we think of as the acceptable pattern of behavior should not matter anymore—only what God says to us in His Word (see Col. 2:8).

Our lifestyle might make us look like idiots before the world. Never mind—that is what makes us peculiar. For instance, the people of the world feel OK about boyfriends and girlfriends living together as though they were married and having sex. We will not do that because our God calls that fornication. Others go to pubs and wile away time for pleasure. They drink and are drunk, but we will not do that because God says not to sit in the seat of sinners.

Other people dress to look sexy. They expose their nakedness and think it is cool to appear that way, but we are careful about how we appear in public because our body is called the temple of the living God. We dress moderately, decently, beautifully, and respectably. While others celebrate in all-night wild parties and are drunk with wine, we do not. We celebrate in worship of God and are filled with the Holy Spirit.

When some worldly people are overpaid, they do not make a refund. They call it luck, and they call the victim an idiot. We will not do such things, because God says that is stealing. All such people are concerned about is what gives them pleasure and satisfaction. What is important to us is what makes God happy, and we lay down our lives for Him. The world does not want to be rebuked, corrected, or instructed—they want to do anything that they feel like doing and call it freedom. We are not to be like that; our lives must be completely surrendered to the lordship of Jesus. His Word is the authority and it is final, and we must order our lives by it.

We must be submitted to leadership for guidance and instruction in righteousness, and we should be willing to give to the Lord anything in sacrifice—even if that will tamper with our pleasure—in gratitude for the gift of life. We are a peculiar people, called out of darkness to show forth the praises of Him who called us. Our lives are lived for His glory, and in the light of His glory everything of this life is as dung.

A HOLY NATION

I beseech you therefore, brethren, by the mercies of God, that ye present your bodies a living sacrifice, holy, acceptable unto God, which is your reasonable service (Romans 12:1).

We are called to live a life of holiness. Holiness simply means to live a life that is in obedience to God. Holiness is about living in the fear of God and ordering our affairs in the light of His Word. Holiness is about doing the will of God. This is true Christianity.

We need to live a holy life because God, who called us into a relationship with Him, is a holy God.

But as He which hath called you is holy, so be ye holy in all manner of conversation; because it is written, Be ye holy; for I am holy. And if ye call on the Father, who without respect of persons judgeth according to every man's work, pass the time of your sojourning here in fear (1 Peter 1:15-17).

We know that for any relationship to work, the people must be in agreement just as the Bible has said (see Amos 3:3). We cannot have a good relationship with a holy God and live an ungodly life, because He is a holy God and He called us to a life of holiness. Holiness and ungodliness cannot fellowship together.

For God hath not called us unto uncleanness, but unto holiness. He therefore that despiseth, despiseth not man, but God, who hath also given unto us His Holy Spirit (1 Thessalonians 4:7-8).

We need to live a holy life because sin no longer has power over us. Actually, our redemption broke sin's power over us. If you are born again, you are a holy man or woman, and God no longer sees you as a sinner but as a holy person. You've got what it takes to manifest a holy life. The Bible puts it this way:

Wherefore, holy brethren, partakers of the heavenly calling... (Hebrews 3:1).

By virtue of our new birth, we receive the nature of God inside us. The man inside us is holy. When we live a holy life, we are just being ourselves. It is our character—the nature of God inside us manifesting on the outside.

Living a holy life shows that we have the fear of God. Redemption empowered us to be who God intended us to be, it did not take away our ability to exercise our will. We can choose to live any lifestyle that we want. When we choose a godly lifestyle, we show that we have respect for God and fear God. Our body is the temple of God; we have got to treat it as sacred and lead it in the fear of God. When we do not do that, we are disregarding God who dwells inside us, and we are showing that we do not have the fear of God.

> *Know ye not that ye are the temple of God, and that the Spirit of God dwelleth in you? If any man defile the temple of God, him shall God destroy; for the temple of God is holy, which temple ye are* (1 Corinthians 3:16-17).

We must live a holy life because without holiness the Bible says no man shall see God. You cannot enjoy a good relationship with God if you are unholy. You can't experience His glory or walk in His power if you are unholy. To see God being involved in a practical way in your life and situation you must live a holy life.

Also, there is no such thing as "once saved, always saved." This would mean that we could behave in any way and still be fine with God. The fact is that if you are not holy at the time of Jesus' return, you will not see God. Don't let anybody lie to you that it does not matter how you live your life—that if you go to church weekly, read the Bible, pray, and give offerings and tithes that is enough. Without holiness, you can't experience God and you can't go to Heaven. Here are a couple of Scriptures that confirm that.

> *Know ye not that the unrighteous shall not inherit the Kingdom of God? Be not deceived: neither fornicators, nor idolaters, nor adulterers, nor effeminate, nor abusers of themselves with mankind, nor thieves, nor covetous, nor drunkards, nor*

revilers, nor extortioners, shall inherit the Kingdom of God (1 Corinthians 6:9-10).

Now the works of the flesh are manifest, which are these; Adultery, fornication, uncleanness, lasciviousness, idolatry, witchcraft, hatred, variance, emulations, wrath, strife, seditions, heresies, envyings, murders, drunkenness, revellings, and such like: of the which I tell you before, as I have also told you in time past, that they which do such things shall not inherit the Kingdom of God (Galatians 5:19-21).

If you are born again, you have eternal life—the life of God in you. You have the ability of God and you can do all things. You have all it takes to manifest all that God has said you are. God's greatest desire is to present us to Himself holy and blameless (see Col. 1:21-23).

THE WAY OF HOLINESS

Being holy is not about observing rules, going to church, reading your Bible, fasting, and all the religious activities that we do. That is not to say that we do not do those things—no, they are godly virtues. Church attendance, the studying of the Word, fasting, and praying without ceasing as God says to do will help us on the road to holiness. However, there are steps to living a life of holiness.

The first step is obedience. Obedience is the road to holiness. God is not only our Father, He is also our Lord and Master. When we made Him our Lord, we declared that He has power and authority over our lives and affairs. We must therefore learn to listen to His Word and follow as He says. We walk in holiness as we follow His leading in our lives.

The second step to a life of holiness is to understand and follow God's rules of godliness. There are rules or laws in the Word, given to us to enable us to achieve holiness.

THE LAW OF TAKING HEED

Wherefore let him that thinketh he standeth take heed lest he fall
(1 Corinthians 10:12).

To "take heed" means to pay attention, to watch out, to be on guard, or to be cautious. I believe that the first thing to watch out for as a believer is that you do not forget that, though you are born again, you are still flesh and blood and the devil is constantly seeking to pull you down. The second thing is that you need to be aware that you have no power, no wisdom, and nothing of your own that can help you overcome the enemy, satan. You must always remember that you can only stand by the grace of God. The day you forget that you are merely human, able to fall, and in need of God to uphold you—that very day will mark the beginning of your descent.

You must also know that there is no spiritual level that you are ever going to get to that will put you beyond falling. If there were such a level, God would not have said, "Let him that thinketh he standeth take heed lest he fall." If you can only remember that you need God to see you through this race, it will help you not to lean or depend on your capability or on your strength. It will help you to trust God every step of the way.

THE LAW OF GIVING NO PLACE TO THE DEVIL

Neither give place to the devil (Ephesians 4:27).

To give no place to the devil simply means to give the devil no advantage or opportunity in your life. All the devil is looking for in anybody's life is an opportunity—just a chance. Until we give him that chance, he can do us no harm. One of the chances he is looking for is when he can get you isolated. Do not let the devil keep you back from the place, thing, or people you are meant to be with at the time you should. If he can isolate you, he can harm you. Do not let him keep you isolated. Remember David and Bathsheba? (See 2 Samuel 11:1-5.) The devil succeeded in isolating David from the battle and then knocked him down.

Another chance satan is looking for is for you to put yourself in the line of temptation. You may think that it does not really matter if you are in a room all alone with your fiancé at the wrong time. You may also think that there is nothing wrong with kissing and cuddling each other, but it can lead to something you have not bargained for. You may think that there is nothing wrong with having the opposite sex as your prayer partner and getting together sometimes in an isolated and enclosed place for prayers. But that might be the chance that satan is looking for. Remember, David did not plan to sleep with Bathsheba.

THE LAW OF FLEEING

There are three fundamental things believers must always flee from. In these areas, we are not called to confront or engage in warfare, but to simply flee.

We Are to Flee From the Appearance of Evil

Stay away from every kind of evil (1 Thessalonians 5:22 NLT).

Something may not really be a sinful thing to do, but the moment it appears either to you or to the people that are around you to be evil, you are to keep away from it. For example, avoid staying in a dark corner or in a room alone with a person of the opposite sex. It is not healthy for a Christian to be involved in a relationship with somebody who is not born again. You may find yourself compromising and doing what you never thought you could do. You are more likely to fall into sin in a relationship with an unbeliever than you are with a believer.

We Are to Flee Youthful Lust

Run from anything that stimulates youthful lusts. Instead, pursue righteous living, faithfulness, love, and peace. Enjoy the companionship of those who call on the Lord with pure hearts (2 Timothy 2:22 NLT).

Youthful lust involves the craze for fame, acceptance, boyfriends or girlfriends, wealth, fashion, and money. Do not allow your life to be centered on that.

We Are to Flee Sexual Sin

Run away from sexual sin! No other sin so clearly affects the body as this one does. For sexual immorality is a sin against your own body. Don't you realize that your body is the temple of the Holy Spirit, who lives in you and was given to you by God? You do not belong to yourself, for God bought you with a high price. So you must honor God with your body (1 Corinthians 6:18-20 NLT).

As a young person who desires to live for God, to flee sexual sin you need to keep away from bad influences. If you are single and do not want to have sex before marriage, then do not date an unbeliever. I have yet to meet an unbeliever who will want to date a lady and not want to have sex with her. An unbeliever does not see anything wrong with having sex before marriage.

If you are in a relationship with a believer who keeps asking you for sex and if you are ready for marriage, get married. But if you are not ready, break the relationship. It is better to break a relationship and lose a friend than losing the comfort of God's Presence. If you are married and do not want to fall into sexual sin, avoid building unhealthy relationships with a person of the opposite sex. To achieve that:

- Never spend more time with someone of the opposite sex than you do with your spouse; if you do, you are giving the devil a chance.

- Never make someone of the opposite sex your best friend or close confidant besides your spouse.

- Never enjoy the comfort of someone of the opposite sex more than you enjoy your spouse's. You are in danger of falling into sin when you notice that you are willing and excited to do something for another woman or man that you are reluctant to do for your spouse. It is also dangerous if you feel you are starting to like that person's company more than your spouse's company. If you realize that you are starting to love the comfort of another man or woman more than your spouse, withdraw from that person. If you do not, you will be giving the devil a chance.

- Never give to a member of the opposite sex a gift that you cannot or have never given to your spouse.

Remember that you are not to stand up to or try to resist the things that God said to flee from. God said to *flee*. Do not try to rebuke the devil or cast him out there. The only way to fight and overcome the devil in those areas is to flee. The Bible says that one cannot play with fire and not be burned (Prov. 6:27-28).

Speaking to the young and unmarried regarding having a boyfriend or girlfriend, I must say that I am of the opinion that it is not a good idea for any brother or sister to have a serious relationship with the opposite sex if he or she is not ready for and is not thinking about marriage. You may find yourself starting to do what you are not supposed to do as a Christian if you become too intimate. Also, do not start a relationship with anybody if he or she is not somebody you can spend the rest of your life with. I believe that it is not healthy for a Christian who is not married to be seen hugging and kissing somebody simply because he or she is in courtship with the person. That can lead to something you do not want to do.

Chapter Six

Knowing and Walking in the Fullness of God

And to know the love of Christ, which passeth knowledge, that ye might be filled with all the fullness of God (Ephesians 3:19).

By *"the fullness of God,"* Paul means having an understanding of God in a deeper way than we do right now. He means to operate at a higher level with God, to be filled with the power of God, and to partake of all that there is for us to partake of in God. When we are filled with the fullness of God, we will operate in the fullness of joy. We will walk in victory over attacks of sickness and disease, defeat and failure, and fear and the power of death, and we will operate on a level of higher knowledge, wisdom, and power.

In the fullness of God, satan cannot stop our advancement. We will desire a thing that God has promised, and it shall come to pass. We will make declarations which will come to pass, for our words will be full of God's anointing. In the fullness of God, we operate above loneliness and depression, the enemy is subjugated, and our expectations come to pass. How do we experience the fullness of God?

KNOW AND RECEIVE THE LOVE OF GOD

You must know that God loves you a lot and His love for you is unconditional. "Unconditional" means that we cannot earn His love and we cannot make Him stop loving us. He loves you just as you are.

We must never think that by living right, giving to the poor, or doing the work of the ministry we can make God love us more. Even without all that He loves us all the same. When we do all the right things, they are for our own benefit, not for God's benefit. Nothing we do can change God in any way, whether good or bad. What we do can only affect us and those around us.

RECEIVE GOD'S FORGIVENESS

You must know that there is nothing you can ever do that God cannot forgive you for. God loves you so much that Jesus died for you, and His love covers all sins. God promised to forgive us of our sin when we ask Him for forgiveness:

If we confess our sins, He is faithful and just to forgive us our sins, and to cleanse us from all unrighteousness (1 John 1:9).

The problem isn't whether God can forgive you, it is whether you can stand to be forgiven. There is nothing that you can ever do that God cannot forgive. You have to learn to accept His forgiveness by forgiving yourself, letting go of the past, and looking to the future.

DEAL WITH GUILT AND SELF-CONDEMNATION

I have seen many believers live in guilt and condemnation. They put themselves in a position where they can't enjoy God—they don't know how to receive God's forgiveness. They allow the devil to continue to use their past to stand in their way. They need to know that when God forgives us, He wipes out all record of our past and treats us like we have never sinned before.

I, even I, am He that blotteth out thy transgressions for Mine own sake, and will not remember thy sins (Isaiah 43:25).

God never condemns—He convicts and He justifies. But He will never condemn His children. Please know that that feeling of condemnation and unworthiness is not from God (see Rom. 8:1).

If you are feeling like God could never love you or reach out and touch you, know that that feeling is from satan. The feeling of guilt and condemnation is not from God. The devil is the accuser of the brethren (see Rev. 12:9-11). The accuser would like to accuse you of everything—even the things that are in the past which God does not have a record of anymore—just to make you walk in guilt and feel dirty and unqualified of anything good that comes from God. He knows that as long as you feel condemned, you are not going to have a fantastic relationship with God. Your prayer life will not be great, and you are not going to be able to walk in faith.

As a born-again child of God, you are not to be sin-conscious but righteousness-conscious. When you sin, repent and receive God's forgiveness and treat it as if it is in the past. When you cannot remember anything sinful in your life, do not start saying, "God, if there be any sin in me, please forgive me." You are only being sin-conscious when you relate to God that way. God wants you to be righteousness-conscious. Any sin you commit unknowingly in fellowship, the blood of Jesus will wash clean.

If we say that we have fellowship with Him, and walk in darkness, we lie, and do not the truth: but if we walk in the light, as He is in the light, we have fellowship one with another, and the blood of Jesus Christ His Son cleanseth us from all sin (1 John 1:6-7).

That is why you must not neglect the fellowship of the brethren. You can only overcome the accuser by confessing that you are the righteousness of God when satan reminds you of things that are in your past. The blood of the Lamb cleanses you, even when you do not confess a sin because you are not aware of it. Let the devil know that there is no enmity between you and God, that you are walking in the light, in fellowship with the brethren, and therefore the blood of Jesus washes you clean and you are not going to walk in condemnation.

WALK CONSCIOUS OF HIS GOODNESS

God's thoughts toward you are good and not evil. He will never do anything to harm you or lead you to do anything that will bring you shame. He will never stand in your way except for your good; He will never put sickness on you or shut the door to destiny against you. God has your interests at heart.

> *For I know the thoughts that I think toward you, saith the Lord, thoughts of peace, and not of evil, to give you an expected end* (Jeremiah 29:11).

God is happy when you are prospering according to His plan—when you are fulfilling your purpose and are fulfilled in life. He is happy when your marriage is blessed, your business is thriving, you are in control of your finances, and you are becoming a blessing.

> *Let them shout for joy, and be glad, that favor my righteous cause: yea, let them say continually, Let the Lord be magnified, which hath pleasure in the prosperity of His servant* (Psalm 35:27).

God is a Father and He thinks well of you—you must be convinced about that. You must believe that God will never give you a heart attack to teach you a lesson, make you go bankrupt to make you humble, make you have a miscarriage to teach you the need to listen to Him, or put sickness on you to slow you down. He will not take away your job, spouse, or children to punish you, and He will not make you have a car crash, lose an eye, or become paralyzed to discipline you. Evil does not come from God and He will not do you harm. The Bible says:

> *Do not err, my beloved brethren. Every good gift and every perfect gift is from above, and cometh down from the Father of lights, with whom is no variableness, neither shadow of turning* (James 1:16-17).

Yes, God chastises those He loves. However, chastisement means that He will convict you of sin—He may take away your peace to bring you to repentance or expose your sin to bring you to godly sorrow. You may not hear the voice of the Spirit like before, and your prayers may be hindered. But He will not harm you. He may allow something that we see as a bad thing to happen. He will not be the cause of it, but He may allow it because He wants to use it to bring about something good for us and in us.

ALLOW CHRIST TO BE FORMED IN YOU

God desires that we be filled with His fullness, and in Christ is the fullness of God.

> *For in him dwelleth all the fullness of the Godhead bodily. And ye are complete in Him, which is the Head of all principality and power* (Colossians 2:9-10).

In Christ dwells the fullness of God. So when Christ is formed in us, we will be filled with His fullness and become complete. Only in Christ are we complete. Being united with Christ is more than just accepting Him as Lord; He needs to be formed in us (see Gal. 4:19). For Christ to be formed in us means that we grow in character and become more like Christ (see Eph. 4:13). A believer's ultimate goal in life should be to be more like Christ. We are to be like Christ in our thinking, our character, and our dealings with people. Paul says:

> *I am crucified with Christ: nevertheless I live; yet not I, but Christ liveth in me: and the life which I now live in the flesh I live by the faith of the Son of God, who loved me, and gave Himself for me* (Galatians 2:20).

People should look at us and be able to see Jesus. It is a problem if people can't see Jesus in the things that we show. To be more like Christ, we must renew our mind and have the mind of Christ. If Christ is formed in us, we will have the mind of Christ (see Phil. 2:5). To have a clear understanding of what that means, let's look at the following Scripture verses.

Let this mind be in you, which was also in Christ Jesus: who, being in the form of God, thought it not robbery to be equal with God: but made Himself of no reputation, and took upon Him the form of a servant, and was made in the likeness of men: and being found in fashion as a Man, He humbled Himself, and became obedient unto death, even the death of the Cross (Philippians 2:5-8).

From the above verses, there are four things we can see in a man when he has the mind of Christ or Christ is formed in him.

THE HUMILITY OF CHRIST

We saw that for Christ, His background, His status, and His achievements did not go to His head. He made Himself of no reputation. He was not particular about His attainment. To gain Christ, we must all do what Paul did to gain Christ. For he writes:

But what things were gain to me, those I counted loss for Christ. Yea doubtless, and I count all things but loss for the excellency of the knowledge of Christ Jesus my Lord: for whom I have suffered the loss of all things, and do count them but dung, that I may win Christ, and be found in Him, not having mine own righteousness, which is of the law, but that which is through the faith of Christ, the righteousness which is of God by faith: that I may know Him, and the power of His resurrection, and the fellowship of His sufferings, being made conformable unto His death; if by any means I might attain unto the resurrection of the dead (Philippians 3:7-11).

Some people think that they are so important that certain classes of people cannot relate to them. They are very conscious of what they have achieved or the family they are coming from, and they think that nobody can talk to them anyway.

Christ was not particular about His status. He was God the Creator, but when He wanted to become human, He chose to come as carpenter and not as one of the nation's senators. When He was going to be born, He chose a stable, not one of the five-star hotels. In dealing with men, He went to dine with tax collectors and sinners in order to influence them. He allowed the harlot to touch Him and to anoint Him with oil. He attracted the leper, the cripple, and the blind. He called them to be His ambassadors—those He was going to train and send out to represent Him. He surrounded Himself with twelve people, most of whom had no education or social standing, and He called them His disciples. That is the mind of Christ.

SERVANTHOOD

There is no humility in your service when you are only able to serve people who are above you or whom you consider to be equals. True humility is seen when you are able to serve those who are nowhere near your level of achievement. Jesus, though He was God, took upon Himself the form of a man and made Himself a servant. This is what it means for Christ to be formed in you. The Spirit of Christ is the Spirit of service; you cannot be part of Christ and not serve.

OBEDIENCE TO GOD

If you are truly following Christ, you are not going to serve God only on your terms or when it suits you. Walking in obedience to God has nothing to do with your happiness. I have heard people say, "I am not happy to do this." Happiness is about your feeling and your situation. Following God is not about that. A lot of the things God will ask us to do will be things that human beings are naturally not happy doing because of their body of sin. But in the nature of Christ, we are willing and excited to obey God even when there is a high price to pay.

The Bible says Jesus was obedient unto death. Dying on the Cross was not something Jesus was excited about, for He asked the Father three times to let the cup pass over. But He still accepted the Father's will and died the death of the Cross. For He said, "…not as I will, but as Thou wilt" (see Matt. 26:39). As a matter of fact, it is recorded that Jesus learned obedience by the things He suffered. He only did what the Father wanted, not what He wanted (see Heb. 5:7-9). And

He said, "…If any man will come after Me, let him deny himself, and take up his cross, and follow Me" (Matt. 16:24).

NOT REVILING BACK

The idea of praying for your enemy to die is not Christlike. The idea of paying back evil for evil is not Christlike. For the Bible says of Him:

> *Who, when He was reviled, reviled not again; when He suffered, He threatened not; but committed Himself to Him that judgeth righteously* (1 Peter 2:23).

It should not surprise you when people rise against you, speak evil of you, or stand in your way. You cannot stop people from thinking what they want to think about you or saying what they want to say about you. But you must never pay back evil for evil—it is not the Spirit of Christ.

> *See that none render evil for evil unto any man; but ever follow that which is good, both among yourselves, and to all men* (1 Thessalonians 5:15).

I pray that, as you read this book, you will let the Holy Spirit work in you, empower you, and help you start to view and relate to people differently, irrespective of what they are doing to you. I pray you will walk by love and in love over the darkness that is around you. You cannot overcome evil with evil but with good only.

Chapter Seven

Walking in Kingdom Authority

And the devil, taking Him up into an high mountain, shewed unto Him all the kingdoms of the world in a moment of time. And the devil said unto Him, All this power will I give Thee, and the glory of them: for that is delivered unto me; and to whomsoever I will I give it. If Thou therefore wilt worship me, all shall be Thine. And Jesus answered and said unto him, Get thee behind Me, Satan: for it is written, Thou shalt worship the Lord thy God, and Him only shalt thou serve (Luke 4:5-8).

Think about the above passage. Was the devil lying when he made that statement to Jesus? I think he was not lying about his lordship of the world, because through the Fall, Adam had delivered to the devil his leadership over what God had committed to him. Even Jesus called satan the prince of this world. But we know that Jesus by His death took back what satan stole from Adam, for the Bible says:

Forasmuch then as the children are partakers of flesh and blood, He also Himself likewise took part of the same; that through death He might destroy Him that had the power of death, that is, the devil; and deliver them who through fear of death were all their lifetime subject to bondage (Hebrews 2:14-15).

Through death, Jesus broke and ended the devil's bondage. In His death, He striped the devil of that authority he stole from Adam. When He told His disciples to *go*, He was saying, "You can now reach out and be an influence. You are now My representatives, and you now function under My authority." The moment you give your life to Jesus, you become a Kingdom man or woman. That puts the devil under your feet (see Eph. 1:17-23). To walk in authority, you must know the level to which God has lifted you in Christ Jesus. You must know your rights in Christ Jesus and be aware of the power of the Holy Spirit available to you. Now let's look at these in more detail.

YOUR HERITAGE IN CHRIST

Therefore if any man be in Christ, he is a new creature: old things are passed away; behold, all things are become new. And all things are of God, who hath reconciled us to Himself by Jesus Christ, and hath given to us the ministry of reconciliation (2 Corinthians 5:17-18).

The death and resurrection of Jesus and our faith in the work of redemption has made us the new creation. The new creation is the wonder of God, the mystery behind the incarnation and the Cross, and the mystery behind the tabernacle in Heaven and the blood of sprinkling. The mystery behind the Man, Jesus, was God's eternal plan to make human beings a new creation. Understand the implication of this and the benefit of the new creation. If you don't, you are never going to fully realize what it made you, what power you carry, and the extent of what you can achieve through Christ (see Luke 10:18-20).

The first thing to be fully aware of is the fact that to the new creation, satan is fallen and no longer has any authority. All power in Heaven and earth is given to Jesus—He took it back and disgraced the devil openly, and Jesus wants us to walk in it. To take your covenant place in the Kingdom and walk in that authority starts with a few steps.

- Understand what Jesus accomplished for you.

- Have a deep understanding of who you are in Christ Jesus and what rights that bestows on you.

- Be aware of the power of the Holy Spirit available to you.

- Know and walk in the consciousness that satan has fallen and lost his authority.

You must be established in this knowledge to walk in authority. Knowing who you are in Christ is important—you are liberated by the redemptive work of Christ and what He has made available to you. What matters in Kingdom authority is not who your parents are, your nationality or race, which part of town you were born and raised in, or what you have achieved. Your degrees, titles, and wealth do not count. It is about who you are in Christ Jesus, who God says you are because of what Jesus did for you, and how you respond to that knowledge.

Do you know who you are in Christ Jesus? Do you know who God says you are because of what Jesus did for you? Do you know what is made available to you because of your relationship with Him? It is very important that you know. When you know, it will make you bold in life; it will completely take fear away from you, especially the fear of death. You will not worry about the devil, the enemy, or the future, and you will live like you are a king. Now let me show you how God sees you.

REDEEMED FROM THE CURSE
OF THE LAW

Christ hath redeemed us from the curse of the law, being made a curse for us: for it is written, Cursed is every one that hangeth on a tree (Galatians 3:13).

There is a lot about redemption that we need to grasp. Redemption means that God no longer has anything against you, not because you have never sinned, but because Jesus paid for all your sins in full. That means that the believer, in redemption, is now the righteousness of God. He qualifies to appear before God and can now stand before

God without the feelings of guilt, condemnation, or inferiority. You are justified and you have peace with God.

> *Therefore being justified by faith, we have peace with God through our Lord Jesus Christ: by whom also we have access by faith into this grace wherein we stand, and rejoice in hope of the glory of God* (Romans 5:1-2).

Redemption means that the believer now has eternal life working in him. He is no longer under bondage to sin, sickness, and disease. Having eternal life is not something to pray about—it is a reality that has happened to whoever has given his life to Jesus; he only needs to believe it, receive it by faith, and walk in the consciousness of it. You have eternal life in you (see 1 John 5:10-12). Eternal life means that the nature of God is imparted to the believer so he can share in the likeness of God. Without eternal life imparted to the believer, he cannot be a child of God.

The believer's body is not to be dominated by sin, sickness, and disease anymore. He is no longer under any form of curse. If someone curses him, the curse has no power. To be free from the curse also means that anything in your past which had power to hurt you and interrupt your destiny has been destroyed. You are now in the blessing and have the power to fulfill God's purpose for your life. There is no more limitation before you.

DELIVERED FROM DARKNESS, TRANSLATED INTO LIGHT

Who hath delivered us from the power of darkness, and hath translated us into the Kingdom of His dear Son (Colossians 1:13).

That you are now in the Kingdom of Jesus means you are no longer under the authority of satan—he lost control over you the day Jesus came into your life. So to think that the enemy can still touch you is ignorant. To think that you can still be possessed of demons and that the devil can easily touch your life and kill you is untrue. To be in the Kingdom of Jesus means you are now a child of the Kingdom. Heaven is now in control of your destiny—Heaven determines your well-being, not the devil. Satan cannot interrupt your destiny; just realize who you are in Jesus and where God has put satan with respect to you.

Satan cannot decide your future, what you can become in life, or how high you can rise. He has no power to shut a door against you or hinder your progress. It is not the government of satan that determines your well-being—he lost that control the day you got transferred from his kingdom to the Kingdom of Jesus. The Kingdom of Jesus is now in full charge of your life—that devil is a liar.

Some of you are walking in fear that you may miss Heaven because satan may overpower you, but you won't. You are already in the Kingdom—your name is in the Book of Life. Satan cannot take you out; he has no power to do that. It is only you who can choose to walk away, just like the prodigal son did. Also, that you are in the Kingdom of Jesus means that you are an ambassador for Christ here on earth.

> *Now then we are ambassadors for Christ, as though God did beseech you by us: we pray you in Christ's stead, be ye reconciled to God* (2 Corinthians 5:20).

An ambassador represents Heaven wherever they go. You have the full backing of the Kingdom of Jesus wherever you are, and that is why satan cannot kill you. Heaven watches over you to protect you and to make whatever you say an authority. When your words line up with God's Word, they are authoritative. Do not take your decrees lightly. Believe me, anybody who touches you or is seeking to harm you is offending God and asking for a fight. That is why He says not to repay, vengeance is the Lord's (see Deut. 32:35). Never fight with another who is in covenant with God. God will defend him.

SEATED WITH CHRIST

> *Even when we were dead in sins, hath quickened us together with Christ, (by grace ye are saved;) and hath raised us up together, and made us sit together in heavenly places in Christ*

Jesus: that in the ages to come He might shew the exceeding riches of His grace in His kindness toward us through Christ Jesus (Ephesians 2:5-7).

To understand how high you are lifted, you need to understand where Christ is seated, for you are seated with Him also. There is no better way to put it than Paul did in Ephesians:

Which He wrought in Christ, when He raised Him from the dead, and set Him at His own right hand in the heavenly places, far above all principality, and power, and might, and dominion, and every name that is named, not only in this world, but also in that which is to come: and hath put all things under His feet, and gave Him to be the head over all things to the Church, which is His Body, the fullness of Him that filleth all in all (Ephesians 1:20-23).

Please underline *"far above all principality, and power, and might, and dominion, and every name that is named"* in your Bible. If Christ is seated far above principality and power and you are seated in Him, where are you seated? If you are seated with Jesus, it means then that the devil and all demon spirits and their human agents are under your feet. By being in Christ, we are elevated above satan and demon spirits and witchcraft powers and all forces of evil—that was the position Adam had before the Fall.

We now can exercise authority over satan and his evil spirits; we can cast out evil spirits and lay hands on the sick and see them healed. We can even drink poison and not be harmed. We are not to fear satan and what he is planning. Satan should fear the new creation. Every born-again person has the authority to cast out devils (see Mark 16:17). You can cast him out wherever you see him. You can command him to leave your finances, your marriage, your work place, and your children. You can cast him out of everything—you have the spiritual and legal oversight.

JOINT HEIR WITH CHRIST

The Spirit itself beareth witness with our spirit, that we are the children of God: and if children, then heirs; heirs of God, and joint-heirs with Christ; if so be that we suffer with Him, that we may be also glorified together (Romans 8:16-17).

Being an heir means that God has something for you to inherit and He has drawn out a will with your name in it. He has a plan for you—He will not withhold anything good from you (see Jer. 29:11). Now if your inheritance is in God's will, you need to understand the will of God because everything that God does is according to the will. There is a document or a book in Heaven with your name on it. In that book, there is something written concerning you. Believe me, there is a book of will in Heaven (see Eph. 1:9-11). You have got to know what is in the will to receive anything from God. Your prayers are not answered when what you are praying for is not in the will (see 1 John 5:14-15).

If only your prayers will line up with the will of God for you, then all your prayers will be answered. Prayers are unanswered either because they don't agree with the will or the person praying is not walking in the light of the covenant. God will always answer when you ask for what is yours. Jesus showed us that in the story he told of the prodigal son (see Luke 15:11-13). The father could not have said no to his son's request, because he was asking in line with their custom and for that which was legally his. Did the father know that he was going to waste his own inheritance? Yes, he did, and he still gave it to him.

The will was written before you were born. Jesus is the testator; He died to activate the will.

For where there is a [last] will and testament involved, the death of the one who made it must be established, for a will and testament is valid and takes effect only at death, since it has no force or legal power as long as the one who made it is alive (Hebrews 9:16-17 AMP).

You might ask, "How do I know what is in the will for me?" Well, the Bible says God put His Spirit inside us so we can know what is in the will for us. With the help of the Holy Spirit, the believer can know the will of God for his or her life. God desires to bless us, answer our prayers, and see us walk in the full knowledge of what He has made available for us so that we will partake of His goodness. Through His Spirit we can know all things (see 1 Cor. 2:9-12). To know what is in the will for you, you need the help of the Holy Spirit. To understand how the Holy Spirit speaks, you must develop your relationship with the Holy Spirit. You need to train your spirit to fellowship with, understand, and walk with Him.

As an heir, God will defend and protect you. As an heir, angels are your servants—they are your ministering spirits. They will be by your side wherever you go and will pave the way for you, rolling every obstacle out of the way (see Heb. 1:13-14). There is no limitation before you—angels now surround you to protect you from evil. You will never be alone no matter where you are. You can send angels on assignment. You can release them to assist you.

Now it is very important to note that the Bible did not only call you God's heir, it says you are a joint heir with Jesus. As a joint heir with Jesus, it means that God will treat you like He treats Jesus. Your value to God is equivalent to how much He values Jesus. You must always remember that you are a special person to God. He has numbered your hairs, and He wrote your names on the palm of His hand. He says you are the apple of His eye (see Zech. 2:8). God will go all out to defend you and make everything you are ever going to go through in life work out for your good. He is never careless about you; He will never forget you and will never let the devil decide your well-being or the outcome of your life.

A KING AND A PRIEST

This is very profound. I know we have looked at it earlier, but I choose to mention it again here because it is important that you start to see yourself as a king and a priest and grasp this. Every believer is a priest of God, not only those who are ordained or are called into full-time ministry. You are a priest; He made us all a Kingdom of priests. As priests of God, it means we all can have the right to access the very Presence of God. God is accessible to you—the throne room is open to you—you can personally experience God, know God, and walk with Him. Never allow anybody to make you think that you need somebody to be able to reach out to God.

And remember, as priest, you are primarily called to appear before God and to minister first to Him and to people in the things of God. As priest, you cannot help but worship; it is your spiritual duty. You don't worship because you want Him to bless you, to attract the anointing or His presence, or to be healed. You worship because He is your God and you are a priest.

Your worship is acceptable to God when your motive is right—when your worship is all about Him. As priest, you are also called to be a teacher in things pertaining to God. You are to reach out to the nations for Him. People must know Him through you. Nobody must have any contact with you and not hear about God. Priests are protectors and teachers of the law and so are you (see 2 Tim. 2:2).

As kings, on the other hand, you are to be responsible for the physical affairs of people and exercise dominion on the earth for the benefit of people. The Bible says, "Verily I say unto you, Whatsoever ye shall bind on earth shall be bound in Heaven: and whatsoever ye shall loose on earth shall be loosed in Heaven" (Matt. 18:18). You've got so much power with God—start to take charge and be a blessing to your generation. You can touch lives and make a difference—you are a king on the earth with all the power of Heaven backing you. As king you are to encourage and strengthen the weak. It is out of order to be a discouragement to somebody or to constitute an obstacle on the way of somebody's success. Nobody must fail in life because of you.

As a king you are to meet the needs of people both emotionally and materially. God made us kings so that we can help stop the work of the devil in the lives of people. We are to exercise control over sicknesses, poverty, and any form of oppression of the devil over people. So as you ask God to bless you with more, you should also ask yourself what you did with things that He has already blessed you with. How did you use them to benefit other people? You see, God sometimes first gives us something that He does not want us to keep for ourselves—He wants us to use it for others' benefit. They are seeds, and only on account of them He opens the door for more. We hinder the blessing when we don't use them like He intends us to. That is why the Bible says:

> Whoever can be trusted with very little can also be trusted with much, and whoever is dishonest with very little will also be dishonest with much. So if you have not been trustworthy in handling worldly wealth, who will trust you with true riches? And if you have not been trustworthy with someone else's property, who will give you property of your own? (Luke 16:10-12 NIV)

THE CONFESSION OF THE WORD

You can also exercise your Kingdom authority through the confession and the declaration of the Word. God's authority is released in the spoken word—He sent forth His word and healed them. The word of God is anointed and you have to learn to use it. Nothing happens until the word is released; even God has to send the word first for anything to happen.

> Then they cry unto the Lord in their trouble, and He saveth them out of their distresses. He sent His word, and healed them, and delivered them from their destructions (Psalm 107:19-20).

Words are spiritual forces; they are the most powerful force in the universe. God used them to create the things that exist today. Words can shape a man's destiny, and if used wrongly, they can cause a fire. You may think that only God can make things happen with words. You can, as well, because God made you as gods (see Ps. 82:6). Your word, too, can be spirit and life, but for your word to have any power and make anything good happen, a few things must happen.

1. It must line up with the Scriptures, for the Bible says, "Who is he that saith, and it cometh to pass, when the Lord commandeth it not?" (Lam. 3:37).

2. Like Jesus, you have got to know that your word is a spirit and has life. And you have to speak with the understanding of what it can accomplish.

3. You must learn to speak the word like you know you have authority and with faith. Speak like you know that it will come to pass and not come back to you void. Remember that you are a king, and the Bible says, "Where the word of a king is, there is power: and who may say unto him, What doest thou?" (Eccles. 8:4).

Words are spirit and they contain life. Words can enslave and set free. They can create life and they can cause death. To walk in authority, you need to start to release the word into situations you want to influence. You should not speak what you are thinking or what everybody is saying, but what the word of God is saying. God says what you allow will be allowed in Heaven (see Matt. 18:18). We allow things by what we say.

Many years ago, when I was visiting my home town and staying with my uncle, my dad's immediate older brother died of tuberculosis. Not long after he died, I started to cough, too, and all the symptoms indicated tuberculosis. So I went to see a doctor. (I had to because the ministry I was involved with at the time wanted me to get some tests.) I went for the test and it showed that I had tuberculosis. But I refused to accept it—I rejected the doctor's testimony and continued to declare that, "I am redeemed and cannot have TB." I told the doctor he got it wrong, because I could not have tuberculosis. He thought I was being foolish, but he referred me for a second test. I went for it, and the test came back negative. If I had accepted the doctor's report, maybe TB would have killed me like it did my uncle. There is power in your confession of faith. You become what you say.

USING THE NAME OF JESUS

To a believer, the name of Jesus is like the staff of authority. When Jesus said we can use His name, He meant that any time His name is used He will treat it as though He was saying it Himself and will enforce it. The Bible says at that name every knee will bow (see Phil. 2:9-11). The name of Jesus is also given to us for defence. You can find security and safety in the use of the name. The devil can't stand the name of Jesus. It has the power to deliver, heal, and shield you from every arrow shot against you. Learn to use it when you find yourself under attack or in trouble.

> *The name of the Lord is a strong tower: the righteous runneth into it, and is safe* (Proverbs 18:10).

If the name of Jesus can guarantee us access into the Holy Presence of God, then the devil cannot stand it. Learn to use that name. Many years ago, my older sister and her husband were driving home from work and the driver missed his way and drove them into a big reservoir. My sister was the only person in the car who could not swim. While the others managed to escape the car and swim to the surface, she was sinking and dying. She said she felt herself go down in the water a few times, but at some point she cried out to Jesus and suddenly she started to float like a feather. They came back with torch lights looking for her and found her floating. The name Jesus kept her from sinking. There is power in that name.

In 1993, I visited a leprosy center in a town called Zaria in the northern part of Nigeria, and as I was walking through I passed this guy who was sitting under a tree. As I passed by, I could see his face and fingers—they were all white and covered with sores. I heard the Lord say to me, "I want to heal him; go pray for him." I got to the guy and asked to pray for him. Initially, he would not let me and was a bit unfriendly. But I insisted and reached out with my hands and held him and rebuked the spirit of leprosy in the name of Jesus. I was afraid of what I was doing and nothing happened instantly, but a week later I came to the center again. As I was walking through like before, I saw this guy coming right toward me, laughing. I did not recognize him; I thought I had never met him before. But he told me he was the guy I prayed for the other week. He was completely healed and restored—I could not have recognized him; he was looking remarkably different from the guy I prayed for. There is power in the name of Jesus.

SIMPLE OBEDIENCE

One other way we can exercise our authority in Christ is by walking in obedience to the Word of God. No believer is in any position to overcome the darkness in disobedience to God. Only in obedience are we empowered to confront the darkness and prevail.

(For the weapons of our warfare are not carnal, but mighty through God to the pulling down of strong holds;) Casting down imaginations, and every high thing that exalteth itself against the knowledge of God, and bringing into captivity every thought to the obedience of Christ; and having in a readiness to revenge all disobedience, when your obedience is fulfilled (2 Corinthians 10:4-6).

Obedience is an act of righteousness—it puts us in the position of righteousness, where we need to be to exercise authority over the devil. In disobedience to God, you cannot exercise that Kingdom authority. Disobedience creates in us the feeling of guilt and an evil conscience. The sense of righteousness makes us bold. Without the sense of righteousness, we cannot overcome the enemy, satan. For the purpose of this topic I would like to present to you two kinds of righteousness.

RIGHTEOUSNESS OF FAITH

This righteousness is conferred on you because of your faith in the redemptive work of Jesus, and it has nothing to do with what you did or did not do. You are made righteous simply because of your faith in Jesus.

But now the righteousness of God without the law is manifested, being witnessed by the law and the prophets; even the righteousness of God which is by faith of Jesus Christ unto all and upon all them that believe: for there is no difference: for all have sinned, and come short of the glory of God (Romans 3:21-23).

This righteousness means "right standing" with God. Your faith in Jesus and His redemptive work brings you into right standing with God. Right standing with God means God no longer condemns you—you are accepted as a child of God and all your transgressions are brought under the sacrificed blood of Jesus. Note that you become righteous the moment you come into faith in Jesus and this has nothing to do with your work.

> *For by grace are ye saved through faith; and that not of your-selves: it is the gift of God: not of works, lest any man should boast* (Ephesians 2:8-9).

RIGHTEOUSNESS AS A BY-PRODUCT OF SALVATION

Now this righteousness is about being compliant to the Word of God and the instruction of the Holy Spirit. This is the kind of right-eousness you find in the Old Testament, and believe me, it is still ap-plicable to us today. It is about doing what is right in the sight of God. This is the kind of righteousness described in Ezekiel 3:20-21.

We need the righteousness which is of faith, but we also do need to do the works of righteousness. The righteousness which is of faith makes you one with God. In other words, it makes you a Kingdom man or woman. The righteousness which is through obedience makes you like God, not having a feeling of guilt or an evil conscience. It brings you into the dimension of authority. Anytime you are acting in the light of the written Word as prompted by the Holy Spirit, the devil may attack you, but he cannot kill you.

> *In righteousness shalt thou be established: thou shalt be far from oppression; for thou shalt not fear: and from terror; for it shall not come near thee. Behold, they shall surely gather to-gether, but not by Me: whosoever shall gather together against thee shall fall for thy sake* (Isaiah 54:14-15).

Jesus says:

> *Whosoever cometh to Me, and heareth My sayings, and doeth them, I will shew you to whom he is like: he is like a man which built an house, and digged deep, and laid the foundation on*

126

a rock: and when the flood arose, the stream beat vehemently upon that house, and could not shake it: for it was founded upon a rock. But he that heareth, and doeth not, is like a man that without a foundation built an house upon the earth; against which the stream did beat vehemently, and immediately it fell; and the ruin of that house was great (Luke 6:47-49).

The fact is that not following the leading of the Holy Spirit will not make you any less a child of God or make void your salvation. But you make yourself vulnerable to the arrows of the enemy and you put yourself in a position where you cannot confront darkness. You never win in disobedience. Many born-again people are working under defeat and are wondering why that is so. You cannot ignore what God is saying to do and expect to win. Only following and doing what He says releases the anointing for winning. If you want to remain on the winning side, then you've got to start to listen and do whatever He says to do.

TAKING CHARGE

What I mean by taking charge is—learn to stand your ground and say no to that devil, knowing that you have the backing of the Lord and the devil will give way. Learn to use commanding words. You are a king, remember? You've got to speak to take charge. Speak to that situation and that devil like you know you have the authority to.

Next the devil took Him to the peak of a very high mountain and showed Him all the kingdoms of the world and their glory. "I will give it all to You," he said, "if You will kneel down and worship me." "Get out of here, satan," Jesus told him. "For the Scriptures say, 'You must worship the Lord your God and serve only Him.'" Then the devil went away, and angels came and took care of Jesus (Matthew 4:8-11 NLT).

To take charge, start to use words like:

- Get behind me satan!

- Leave now, in Jesus' name!

- The Lord rebukes you, satan. Go!

- I reject it—that is not my portion.

- Be healed in the name of Jesus.

Now you need to understand that satan cannot be bound as in chaining him down so that he will not be able to move about. You cannot bind him that way. People speak in ignorance when they bind him with that in mind. We can bind him by forbidding him to touch something, but we cannot bind him to stop him from operating generally. Also, you need to understand that you cannot send satan to hell, like some people command in ignorance, until the time appointed to him.

I have heard all kinds of prayer in our churches. I heard somebody praying, "Satan, I break your head with a hammer. I command you to fall down and die." That is ignorance—satan cannot die. I also heard somebody say, "Satan, I send you to the bottomless pit, and I torment you with the fire of hell." It does not work; you must pray in line with the Word to get results. You can cast him out, tell him to leave, and forbid him from touching something. For this to work for you, you must be authoritative—know that you are seated with Christ in the heavenly places far above, and satan is under you. Stand firm on the Word, be bold, be authoritative, and be convinced that it shall be so.

Chapter Eight

The Excellent Spirit

That ye may approve things that are excellent; that ye may be sincere and without offence till the day of Christ (Philippians 1:10).

Being excellent means doing more than what is just good enough. The word "excellent" can be defined as being exceptionally good, first-class, first-rate, splendid, super, or superb. The excellent spirit is a result-oriented spirit. But it is not only that—it also strives for the *best* result. The excellent spirit is never satisfied with just good—it seeks to achieve the best. I believe that God wants us to all operate in the excellent spirit, because He is an excellent God. The Bible says, "Be ye therefore followers of God, as dear children" (Eph. 5:1). I also believe that for us to achieve any greatness, to affect our environment or community in a positive way, to show forth God's praises, and to leave a mark on the shore of this side of eternity, we will need the excellent spirit.

Daniel was a man the Bible says operated with an excellent spirit (see Dan. 5:11-12). We saw that the excellent spirit made room for him, not his race or his connection to anybody. He became great even in a land where he was a captive. He served in leadership through successive regimes and was held in high esteem. His excellence elevated him above others. If your boss or colleagues are complaining about your performance or the quality of your work, do something about that. Do not just conclude that you are being persecuted because you are a Christian or that you are dealing with racism. Slow down and take a close look at your work.

Everybody appreciates quality and excellence. Nobody likes associating with mediocrity; nobody is proud to be associated with failure. If you are successful, people will want to identify or associate with you. Education is good and we should all pursue education, but what use is your education if it has not helped to enhance the quality of your work? Excellence is about the value you place on life, your attitude toward people, how much you value relationships, and what level of commitment you are willing to make for your relationships. It is also about your attitude toward work and the quality of your output.

Excellence is the highway to achievements. It is difficult to be successful where there is no excellence. A lot of people you see today who are stagnant, not moving forward especially in their career, not achieving anything, or not positively affecting the lives of those around them, I believe, are mostly those who are lazy, satisfied with mediocrity, and OK with a low life, low standard, and low-quality performance. Some are even content with their stagnancy. They do not place much value on growth or progression, and they even think that it is humility to be that way. These sort of people cannot make any meaningful impact in life, not because they are cursed or don't have the ability to make it. They cannot make it because they are not progressive-minded, creative, or innovative—they are just lazy.

I believe that anybody can achieve excellence. You can achieve it, too. I want to present to you some qualities that you will always find in a man or woman with an excellent spirit. You can ask God to help you cultivate these qualities so that you can be the best that you are meant to be.

PEOPLE-ORIENTED MINDSET

Excellence starts with putting value on people. Everything that you do must be to add value to people. I believe that relationships are more important than work or career. Success in relationships outweighs career success or any achievements. An excellent spirit would therefore place more value on building and developing relationships with family members, colleagues, and neighbors first. I believe that a people-oriented mindset will not go for success at all cost or at the expense of relationships. The most important relationship is the one between a husband and wife. In a nutshell, a person who is people-oriented:

- Puts value on people and relationships.

- Enjoys spending time with people more than at work.

- Demonstrates trust and respect, especially for those he is connected with.

- Treats no one as a nobody or inferior.

- His motivation is not always about me and I, but we and us.

SERVANT-ORIENTED MINDSET

Apart from the fact that we are sons of God, we are also called to be servants. A Christian must see himself as a servant of God wherever he is. A true servant lives for his master and not for himself. He puts the master's desire and interests first and not his own interest or desire. All he cares about is how to please his master. A true servant from a Christian perspective is the person whose life has been dedicated or set apart for the service of God, and in serving God he serves humanity. He may not be in a full-time Christian ministry; nevertheless, he sees himself as God's servant first, and he treats every other enterprise that he is involved with as a channel through which he can bring increase to God's Kingdom and glorify Him.

A true servant must be willing to pour himself out in every area of his life. He must be willing and ready at any time to give his life, his time, his talents, his money, his property, and everything he has for God. If God is truly our Master, we should be more concerned about pleasing Him than anything else. We should seek after God more than anything that is in this world, and we should be willing and ready to make any sacrifice for Him, whenever He demands it. Servanthood is one of the things you will see in the excellent spirit, and selflessness is one of the fundamental things you will find in a true servant. Selfless motivation for service is not about what one gets out of it, but how it benefits those who are being served.

A true servant of God does not serve for material benefit or for the name he can make for himself. He does not work for his own interest first, but for the interest of his master. Nor does he seek after his own profit first, but the profit of him he serves. Selflessness puts others' needs first; that is the heart of a servant. When people serve for the sake of what they can gain, you see unhealthy competition—people wanting to rise at someone else's expense and keeping back things that can change somebody's life for good. How can we hesitate to help somebody because he or she might become better than us?

When people serve for what they can gain, you see eye service, or men-pleasers as the Bible puts it—people doing things so they can be noticed and applauded. They get offended if no one thanks them or rewards them. But the Bible says:

> *Servants, obey in all things your masters according to the flesh; not with eyeservice, as menpleasers; but in singleness of heart, fearing God; and whatsoever ye do, do it heartily, as to the Lord, and not unto men* (Colossians 3:22-23).

One of the fundamental things you will notice in a servant's heart is the joy of service. A true servant is happy doing what he is doing, not because of his ability to gain from it, because it is comfortable, or because everybody thinks he is doing a great job. First, it is because he knows that he is serving God, not man. Second, he knows he is contributing by helping other people to be better people. The thought of somebody becoming better is a motivation to the servant heart.

Also, a servant is loyal. Loyalty involves sticking with people both when things are going well and when they turn sour. Loyalty is about sticking up for people and defending them, even when they caused the mess they are in. The people you believe in will always make mistakes, but don't join others to stab them. That is loyalty. It is not about condoning what is wrong—it is about not abandoning them but sticking with them and helping them come out of it. Loyalty is about being available for people when they need you most and making sacrifices for them even when it is costly to do so. You see, loyalty is not demonstrated when the person is looking great and attractive. We demonstrate loyalty when things have turned sour and we are still sticking up for the person. It is always costly to be loyal, but when you are loyal to people, they find value in you. They commit to you, too, and will want to do anything for you.

RESULT/SUCCESS-ORIENTED MINDSET

A man with an excellent spirit has a success mentality. He believes in success. He dreams, sees, and talks about success. He never sees himself failing, only succeeding. That is not to say that he is never going to fail in anything. Even the most successful people in the world today have failed before, but they do not accept or yield to defeat. They sometimes miss it, but they never dwell on it. They often make big pronouncements, so people might think they are proud, but it is not pride—it is their mindset. The difference between these people and those who fail is that they see solutions where a failure sees problems and defeat. They see possibilities where everything suggests the contrary. Failure-oriented people only see the problems, the obstacles, and limitations.

PROGRESSIVE MINDSET

One definite thing that you will always find in a man who is given to excellence is that he craves for more knowledge. He is always seeking and searching to discover new things and new and improved ways of doing things. Actually, it is his continuous learning that has made him an excellent man. There is no limit to knowledge, and you are never too knowledgeable or too old to learn. David Ben-Gurion, the founder of the state of Israel, learned how to speak French when he was seventy years old. The Bible says:

Those that be planted in the house of the Lord shall flourish in the courts of our God. They shall still bring forth fruit in old age; they shall be fat and flourishing (Psalm 92:13-14).

It is your continuous learning and training, whether formal or informal, that will increase your production capacity. Your productivity is motivated when you yield to mental development. To a large extent, what you can do is determined by how much knowledge you have. For instance, if you are doctor, your level of knowledge in medicine will determine the quality of your practice. Never stop learning, because excellence is stirred up inside you through information. Information triggers vision, creativity, and innovation.

ORGANIZATIONAL SKILLS

The person with an excellent spirit has the ability to arrange, put in order, or manage the things that he or she is part of. Such things include the order of things in a person's house (in the lounge, bedroom, or kitchen), the setup in the office, the church setting, et cetera. You can tell a person who is particular about excellence from the look of the kitchen, the way he or she keeps his or her hair (neat or shabby), and her style of dressing. Decency and order is God's standard, as the Bible says:

Let all things be done decently and in order (1 Corinthians 14:40).

One of the excellent things about King Solomon was his ability to put things in order (see 1 Kings 10:1-7). That was what captivated the Queen of Sheba, not his wealth. She observed the way his servants ministered, how they rose and how they sat, how Solomon would sit at his table, and the arrangement of things in his palace and garden. In everything, she was captivated. Excellence is also about order.

EFFICIENCY MINDSET

Efficiency means doing things thoroughly, effectively, and in detail. It means being on top of your skill, doing things cost-effectively, time-effectively, and competently and achieving the best result.

Whatsoever thy hand findeth to do, do it with thy might; for there is no work, nor device, nor knowledge, nor wisdom, in the grave, whither thou goest (Ecclesiastes 9:10).

Believers must aim at developing and improving their skills. They must strive to be the best at what they do. We cannot afford to be shabby, lazy, callous, negligent, unprofessional, and unprofitable in what we do. Always aim to achieve the best result possible, give the best, study hard to understand the job at hand, and look at the details— never assume.

TASTE AND FLARE FOR QUALITY

Something of quality means it is of high standing. It is not mundane, common, or ordinary. An excellent man always goes for the best; he does not settle for anything less. Some people like going for what is cheap and second-grade. They think that is humility. I have learned that it is not— it is either being tight-fisted, having an inferiority complex, or living with a low-life mindset. Excellence goes for what is top grade or of high quality. I am not suggesting to always look for the most expensive things. No, the fact that something is expensive does not necessarily mean that it is high-quality. However, many things that are high-quality can be expensive. Excellence does not usually come cheap.

BOLDNESS

Boldness is a virtue of excellence. It is the demonstration of courage and fearlessness in the face of defeat, challenges, or opposition. Boldness makes people take daring steps in spite of opposition and threats of failure. I believe that boldness is developed out of the conviction that everything is possible with God. Those who are going to make it in life are the people who are willing to confront their fear, doubt, and every negative feeling.

Bold people believe in themselves and in their ability. They are not afraid of failing, and they are not afraid to step into new grounds, because they are persuaded that all things are possible with God. You need boldness to continue in something when it seems like it is not going to work and everybody else thinks you are either stupid or crazy. That boldness is a virtue of the excellent spirit.

COMMITMENT

Commitment is a resolution which an individual makes to stick to a cause, enterprise, or person no matter the circumstances. Excellent people succeed because they commit to everything that they believe in and are part of. Everything in life that people engage in—marriage, relationships, studies, career, church, leadership, or followership— has potential for greatness, but only commitment can bring that greatness out. It does not matter how lucrative your vocation or job is. It could be the hottest thing in town, but if you are not committed to it, it won't make you great. If you are working for someone like me, I will definitely sack you.

It is actually a waste of time to be involved with anything that you do not believe in and know you are not going to commit to. There are two things that show that you are really committed to something. The first is the fact that you are willing to stick with it through thick and thin. The second is that you are willing to make sacrifices and give it anything that you believe it needs to bring forth its fruits.

Chapter Nine

You Are Anointed

Now he which stablisheth us with you in Christ, and hath anointed us, is God; who hath also sealed us, and given the earnest of the Spirit in our hearts (2 Corinthians 1:21-22).

It is important that a child of God should know that he is not only saved, made a new creation, and translated into the Kingdom of Jesus, but God has also anointed him. It is not only men of God or ministers of the Gospel who are anointed—you are anointed, too, if you are born again. God anointed you so that you can rise above your limitations and in every circumstance you can express His nature and His creativity and be what He called and ordained you to be on the earth.

"Anointing" means the ability or enabling power of God. Being the anointed of God means that God has empowered you and has put His ability in your life to enable you to become what He wants you to be. The Bible says, *"I can do all things through Christ which strengtheneth me"* (Phil. 4:13). The word *Christ* here means the Anointed One and His anointing. Through the operation of the anointing you can do all things, achieve anything, overcome anything, become anything, and rise to any height in life. There is no limit before you because of the Anointed One and His anointing which strengthens you. There is something else I would like to show from the Bible:

For it is God which worketh in you both to will and to do of His good pleasure (Philippians 2:13).

If you have a passion or desire to be somebody and to achieve something in life—the kind of passion which will not just go away—that has been put inside of you by God for His own pleasure and for His own glory. To put it in other words, through the workings of the indwelling Holy Spirit in the believer, God always puts a desire for something in us. This desire will fulfill His purpose on the earth. No desire or ambition is evil on its own unless it is channelled toward man or used to gratify one's ego. If it is channeled toward God, it is a noble thing of God. Therefore, your achievement in life and your success in any area should not be the end itself, but a means to fulfilling something God has ordained to be on the earth.

God likes us to be excellent in what we do, to be achievers, and to excel in the things we do. He is happy for you to be the president of your country, the president or the CEO of your company, or the best fashion designer. He wants you to be the first to fly to Mars. He is glorified by your achievements. Mediocrity is not God's idea for you, and if you are a child of God, it is important to quickly realize that God has raised you up and is making something which He has anointed you for. You are God's vessel and a channel of His praise.

You are called of God according to His purpose. There is something in the mind of God concerning you. You are a child of destiny. When you were saved, God put His abilities in you, and now He is giving you specific ideas, desires, visions, dreams, and passions to achieve certain things in life. Now that you have His ability, you can achieve anything; you can rise to any height. Your dream is not beyond you— if you can dream it, you can become it. You cannot afford to fail in your endeavors. It is important to realize that there is no idea, ambition, or dream that you have that is beyond your reach. There is nothing that you can conceive in your heart that is not achievable. So long as you can conceive the idea, you can achieve it because there is an anointing on your life to make it come through. The Bible says:

Now unto Him that is able to do exceeding abundantly above all that we ask or think, according to the power that worketh in us (Ephesians 3:20).

Jesus did not fail, and He could not have failed because He had the anointing (see Acts 10:38). You, too, have the anointing, and you can't fail because of it—you can achieve anything. You can rise to any level. There is nothing that will come your way that you cannot handle. You are anointed so you can achieve the destiny God has given you.

FIVE THINGS THE ANOINTING DOES

I would like you to look at what happened to Saul, the king of Israel, when he was anointed by Samuel the prophet. This can show you what you can experience because of the anointing.

Then Samuel took a vial of oil, and poured it upon his head, and kissed him, and said, Is it not because the Lord hath anointed thee to be captain over His inheritance? When thou art departed from me to day, then thou shalt find two men by Rachel's sepulchre in the border of Benjamin at Zelzah; and they will say unto thee, The asses which thou wentest to seek are found: and, lo, thy father hath left the care of the asses, and sorroweth for you, saying, What shall I do for my son? Then shalt thou go on forward from thence, and thou shalt come to the plain of Tabor, and there shall meet thee three men going up to God to Bethel, one carrying three kids, and another carrying three loaves of bread, and another carrying a bottle of wine: and they will salute thee, and give thee two loaves of bread; which thou shalt receive of their hands. After that thou shalt come to the hill of God, where is the garrison of the Philistines: and it shall come to pass, when thou art come thither to the city, that thou shalt meet a company of prophets coming down from the high place with a psaltery, and a tabret, and a pipe, and a harp, before them; and they shall prophesy: and the Spirit of the Lord will come upon thee, and thou shalt prophesy with them, and shalt be turned into another man. And let it be, when these signs are come unto thee, that thou do as occasion serve thee; for God is with thee. And thou shalt go down before me to Gilgal; and, behold, I will come down unto thee, to offer burnt offerings, and to sacrifice sacrifices of peace offerings: seven days shalt thou tarry, till I come to thee, and shew thee what thou shalt do. And it was so, that when he had turned his back to go from Samuel, God gave him another heart: and all those signs came to pass that day (1 Samuel 10:1-9).

We can take out the following from the account of King Saul's anointing. And remember, this applies to you, too.

1. You are anointed so you can have charge over the treasures and the wealth of the Kingdom (see 1 Sam. 10:1). You are anointed to experience more than enough and to be a blessing.

2. You are anointed so you can have information, answers, solutions, and keys that will unlock situations and circumstances (see 1 Sam. 10:2). As a result of you being anointed, your mind is blessed, you are a man or woman of understanding, you are an informed person, and you can no longer stay in the dark.

3. You are anointed to have favor (see 1 Sam. 10:3-4). Even your enemies can bless you; do not pray for them to die. Expect favor when you are attending an interview, expect favor in a strange land and before strangers, expect favor when you have to answer before a judge. As you read this book I pray that your life will turn around for good, bringing you out of debt and before kings.

4. You are anointed so you can operate in the prophetic (see 1 Sam. 10:6). Because of the anointing of God on your life, whatever you say by faith carries power and authority. Your word is a spirit, and what you say can come to pass because of the anointing.

5. The anointing on you is to prove that God is with you wherever you go (see 1 Sam. 10:7). The Bible says if God

is for us, who can be against us (see Rom. 8:31)? Because God is with you, no evil plotted against you shall prosper, and things that seemed impossible with men will be possible for you (see Matt. 19:26).

WALK IN THE ANOINTING

Now, do not think that because God's anointing is on your life everything about you will work out automatically and that you will not have to fight for anything. All of God's blessings work within a principle. There is something you have got to do to release the anointing on your life.

First, you must believe that you are anointed and always be conscious of that fact. The devil will want to keep you ignorant or make you forget that you are anointed by God. Always remember that you have the ability of God to make it anywhere, anytime, and in anything. Sometimes our problem is not knowing who we are in Christ, but holding on to that knowledge when things get tough, hard, and difficult. God says that if we reject knowledge, He will also reject us (see Hos. 4:6). It is important that you always know that:

- The fact that things are not working out for you right now does not mean that you are not going to make it.

- Having tried once and failed does not mean that you are a failure and cannot succeed.

- If nobody appreciates you or what you are doing, it does not mean that you are a nobody.

- You are somebody with the ability and wisdom of God. You can do all things through Him who strengthens you. But you have to believe it and be conscious of it at all times.

The Bible says that it is not the beginning of a thing that matters, but the end (see Eccles. 7:8). Therefore, things not working out for you now does not mean that you are a failure. If only you can hold on to your belief and your confession, God will confirm you at the end.

If you look at history, you will see that most people who have made it big in life have also struggled at some point in their lives. It is not really how you start in life that matters—it is how you are going to end that matters. The fact that it is rough now does not mean that you will end badly.

The second thing needed to make the anointing work for you is understanding the dimensions of the anointing and how they work. The anointing in your life is in two dimensions.

You are anointed *within*. The Holy Spirit is the anointing, and you have Him on the inside of you (see Rom. 8:8-9,14-16; 1 Cor. 3:16). The anointing within is a teaching or guiding anointing for inspiration and understanding (see John 14:26; 16:12-15; 1 John 2:27).

You are anointed *upon* (see Acts 1:8; Isa. 61:1). This anointing is the doing or the enabling anointing. It is the power to manifest God's abilities in your life (see Phil. 4:13).

The anointing upon and the anointing within work together. The anointing upon is effective in your life only when you follow your spirit, that is, the anointing within. As a believer, you must not labor to be like somebody else or be what somebody wants you to be. You need to learn to listen to what your heart is saying and follow it (see Prov. 18:16; Eph. 4:7). If you ignore the leading of the anointing within, the anointing upon will be hindered. That is why, as a child of God, you should not just follow the opinion or counsel of men, and you should not do anything simply because everybody else is doing it. You must learn to do only what you can sense the Holy Spirit urging you to do. When you follow the anointing within, the anointing upon is released to make what you do prosper.

Third, you must commit to diligence and hard work. The anointing works only when we are dedicated, committed, and hard-working. It does not work for careless and lazy people. When you are not doing anything, the anointing will be empowering and prospering nothing. When you are not committed to anything, the anointing is not activated for anything. God says that those who do not work should not eat (see 2 Thess. 3:10-12). If you are committed, hard-working, and diligent in your endeavors, God will definitely command increase in what you do (see Prov. 10:4; 12:24; 22:29).

The anointing can be released through fasting and prayer. You cannot ignore the place of prayer if you really want to succeed. Jesus had to pray to the Father, so why think that we do not need to pray? If you think so, then you must be more anointed than Jesus. The Bible says to pray without ceasing. When you fast, you suppress the bad habits you have which are working against you—you conquer temptations that the devil is trying to use to bring you down.

The anointing can also be released through the laying on of hands (see Deut. 28:8; Mark 16:17-18). Learn to lay your hands on your head, on your children, and on that thing which represents your job and bless it. You can apply this principle to as many things as you need God's power to bless. Power is released when we do this by faith.

I would like to make it clear here that it is not in line with the Scriptures for anybody to lay his hands on somebody who is superior to him spiritually to bless him. You cannot lay hands on your spiritual mentor or your spiritual father to empower him. I have been to churches where I saw church members or leaders coming to lay hands on their pastor to pray for him as he prepares to go up the pulpit to preach. It is an abnormality; it should not be so at all. The Bible says:

Now beyond all contradiction the lesser is blessed by the better (Hebrews 7:7 NKJV).

When you lay hands on somebody, you are simply saying, "I release into your life what I have in me." It is an empowerment. You do not do that for your leader, your mentor, your teacher, your spiritual father, or somebody that you know is spiritually ahead of you. Anointing does not flow from the toes to the head; it flows from the head down (see Ps. 133:1-3). It is like placing your hand on your natural father and saying, "Father, may God be with you, keep you in life, and make you see good days." The son does not bless the father; the father blesses the son. You can lay your hands on anybody only in the area of sickness, and even then, if you are dealing with somebody you know is spiritually ahead of you, you may need his permission to do that.

THE APPLICATION OF THE WORD
AND THE ANOINTING

Let the word of Christ dwell in you richly in all wisdom;
teaching and admonishing one another in psalms and hymns
and spiritual songs, singing with grace in your hearts to the
Lord (Colossians 3:16).

The greatest gift of God to a believer, after the gift of Jesus and
the Holy Spirit that dwells within him, is the Word of God. Its
importance to us in our relationship with God and our well-being
cannot be overemphasized. The amount of the Word of God that
a believer contains and the revelation he has from it determines his
spiritual strength and his quality of life. Being prayerful alone does
not make anybody spiritually strong. It is the practical application of
the Word and prayer that makes one strong.

Every believer needs to understand the value of the Word, take it
seriously, and commit to it. The Word of God is highly anointed and
powerful. As a matter of fact, there is more anointing in the Word than
there is in the name of Jesus. If there is anything one cannot achieve
by the application of the Word of God, then even the use of the name
of Jesus cannot make it happen, because the Word is magnified above
His name. The Bible says:

I will worship toward Thy holy temple, and praise Thy name
for Thy lovingkindness and for Thy truth: for Thou hast mag-
nified Thy word above all Thy name (Psalm 138:2).

Therefore, the more of the Word we have dwelling inside us, the
more of the revelation of God we are going to have. The more we
increase in the revelation of God, the more the grace of God increases
in our lives, and we will see more results in the things that we do.

Grace and peace be multiplied unto you through the knowledge
of God, and of Jesus our Lord (2 Peter 1:2).

The Word can touch and transform every sphere of our lives if we
let it. The sad thing, though, is that churches teach little of the Word

these days. So we see church folks running after preachers and meetings where hands can be laid on them and anointing oil poured on them. They want to be healed, they seek after prosperity and deliverance, and they want their enemies to die, but their lives are shallow in the Word, and they do not live it. They want revival and miracles but are not passionate about the Word of God. I am not in any way trying to undermine the place of the other types of ministry, but the fact is that we cannot lay aside the Word and be who God wants us to be in the Kingdom. The Word must be the believer's food.

VALUE IN THE WORD

When one gives his life to Christ and is born again, he has become like a newborn baby in the Lord. As a baby will require milk to grow, likewise he needs the Word to grow (see 1 Pet. 1:2). It is important that we grow spiritually, because if we remain babes in Christ, there will be certain blessings which we will not be able to appropriate because they are meant for mature believers only (see Gal. 4:1-3).

- The Word of God is given to us to liberate us from every bondage and oppression (see John 8:30-32).

- The Word is given to us for doctrine, correction, and instruction in righteousness (see 2 Tim. 3:16-17).

- The Word of God is given to us so that through it we can know the will of God, and in knowing it, live a life pleasing to God (see Ps. 119:11,105,130).

- We are given the Word of God so that it can mature us in the things of God and bring us to a place where we qualify to partake of our inheritance in Christ (see Acts 20:32).

- We are given the Word of God so that we can be healed from every sickness and live a healthy life (see Ps. 107:20).

- The Word is given so that we can succeed in what we do and be materially and financially prosperous (see Ps. 1:1-3).

THE SPOKEN WORD OF FAITH

There is power in the spoken word. Learn to speak the Word into every situation of your life. Confess only the Word about yourself, your job, your studies, and your family. No matter the situation, only speak what God has said about you. Don't wait until something starts to go wrong in your life or you are faced with a challenge before you start to make confessions of faith regarding your life. Learn to speak the Word into every situation of your life, even when things are going well with you. When you speak the Word when things are going well, you are engaging in spiritual exercise and your spirit is being developed—you are developing spiritual muscles for the time of adversity. It takes time for the Word to take root in your spirit and bring forth fruit. You need to start to declare the Word into your situation when things are going well—the Word will not only build a tower around you and take root inside you, but it will also develop your faith and prepare you for the time of adversity.

Faith confession is the language of the Kingdom. It is the believer's profession; it is designed to be our lifestyle. You must learn not to speak what you see, feel, or hear, but the Word of God. Usually confession starts from head knowledge, but when you make faith confession a lifestyle, the Word of God will take root in your heart and grow faith in you. When your confession is from your heart, it starts to be accompanied by the anointing of the Spirit. Speak out the Word regarding your finances, health, marriage, and career regularly. Do not wait until you are going through an attack. Never say, "My eye disease," "my heart condition," "my kind of headache, my, my…"—they are not yours, they belong to the devil. Do not claim them for yourself. You must reject every infirmity and every kind of sickness. Also, never make negative confessions like these.

- "I am always broke; it does not look like I am ever going to make it."

- "Anytime I have this feeling, something bad always happens. The way I am feeling now, something bad will happen to me."

- "This exam I am writing is tough. I am not sure I am going to make it."

- "I am always having bad luck with relationships. I do not know why."

- "Why did God allow this to happen to me, why did He not stop it? Maybe I am cursed."

- "This problem—I do not know what to do with it. The way it is going, I hope it does not kill me."

- "My parents are very difficult people to deal with; it is always hard to get anything from them. I cannot even try."

- "The people at my workplace are racists. I do not think I am going to stay there long. If I do not leave, they are only going to mess me up."

- "This country is hard; I really do not know why I am here."

As long as you keep making those unbelieving confessions, you are never going to come out of those situations. Faith confession is not about declaring what your real situation is, it is about declaring what the Word of God has said regarding your situation. To come out of your situation, you have got to start to declare what the Word says. That is the way of the Kingdom, and that is how the anointing is released.

For with the heart man believeth unto righteousness; and with the mouth confession is made unto salvation (Romans 10:10).

You might not be able to keep the devil from putting doubt in your mind, but if in the midst of your doubt you can speak the Word, the doubt will die. If you stop entertaining the devil's doubts and start speaking the Word, you will see a change. It will become natural for you to speak words of life even in the midst of an obstacle. Once you speak contrary to the doubt in your mind, you kill it and break its power over you.

It is an evil report to speak out what the Word of God has not said. You release an evil report to your situation any time you speak contrary to the Word, even if what you are saying is actually the physical reality. Remember the ten spies Moses sent to spy out the land of Canaan? What made what they said an evil report was simply the fact that it contradicted what God told them, not because they said what they did not see. What you say may be your material situation, but if what you are saying is contrary to the Word, then what you are saying is an evil report. The believer must not walk by sight but by faith (see 2 Cor. 5:7). Faith is seeing yourself and your situation in the light of the Word.

FAITH CONFESSION AND FAITH ACTION

Faith confession and idleness do not go together. You cannot idle away your life at home doing nothing and then speak financial breakthrough into your life and expect money to appear in your bank account. Confession of faith is powerful only when you are acting on the Word as well. Faith confession and faith action are a powerful combination. To make your confession on financial breakthrough effective, you will need to get a job. If you are confessing and believing for a job, then keep sending out those applications and keep looking. Also, be faithful in tithing, offering, and sowing seed into the lives of men. Simply confessing that the Lord will supply all your needs according to His riches will not release any anointing if you do not know how to give (see Phil. 4:19). For better health, you will need to start eating healthy food and doing some exercises. For promotion or success, you will need to be diligent and hard-working. If you are lazy and unprofessional at work, you are going to get fired, and the anointing will not prevent it.

DEVELOPING YOUR SPIRITUAL POTENTIAL

But ye, beloved, building up yourselves in your most holy faith, praying in the Holy Ghost (Jude 20).

It is your duty to grow and develop your spirituality. I mean, it is your duty to develop your relationship with God, your understanding of the operations of the Holy Spirit, and your spiritual power or anointing. The Bible says to be strong in the Lord and in the power of His might (see Eph. 6:10). In building yourself up spiritually, you need to know your composition—you are a tripartite being. In other words, you are formed in three parts—you are a spirit, you possess a soul, and you live in a body. You need to understand the body, soul, and spirit in relation to your walk with God and align them appropriately.

THE BODY

The body, which is a container, is flesh and blood. The flesh needs food and water to live (see Matt. 4:4). It also needs sleep, rest, exercises, and cleaning to be healthy and functional. If we neglect the body, it loses strength and becomes sick and ineffective, and it eventually dies. It is our duty to take care of it and nurture it. The Bible says that our body is the temple of God (see 1 Cor. 6:19). God's plan is that our body should be sacred—the expression of His glory.

We are to keep our body holy unto God. In the Old Testament, God dwelt in tabernacles which were built by human hands. In this dispensation, He lives inside men. Human bodies are now His dwelling place. If God lives in your body—and the Bible says He does—then you must consider your body as a sacred thing. You must keep it holy unto the Lord, because God who dwells in it is a holy God (see 1 Cor. 3:16-17; Eph. 1:4; 1 Thess. 4:7-8). When you yield to unrighteousness, you despise God, not man. You are simply telling Him that He has no claim over your body. When you do that, you are fighting God.

WHAT TO DO WITH YOUR BODY

See your body as a sacred place, a home for the presence of the Most High God. Be conscious of that every day, and trust God to help you live a life that shows forth His praise.

To keep your body holy, you must learn to bring it under subjection (see 1 Cor. 9:27; Rom. 12:1-2; 6:13,19). God does not speak or lead His children through the body, so your body must not lead you. Say "no" to its cravings and desires. You can tell the body when to eat and when not to—it must not be the driving force.

You must learn not to overwork the body. You must not kill it, because God will hold you responsible for that. Give it rest when it needs it—that is the purpose of the Sabbath. He gave us the Sabbath so that the body can be rested.

THE SOUL

The soul is that part of man that is responsible for your emotions, intellect, reason, et cetera. While the body can die, the soul lives forever. It does not die. When your body is dead, you are still going to be conscious and have emotions and the sense of reason because the soul lives on.

The soul is a gateway—it receives, interprets, and passes information to the body. The soul receives information either from the worldly realm or from the spiritual realm. The information that the soul transmits to the body determines our actions, so the source of our information determines the type of behavior we exude. If the information is from the spiritual realm, the man becomes spiritual; if it is from the worldly realm, the man becomes carnal. The body is therefore controlled from the realm of the soul. What you feed your mind with will determine your behavior.

WHAT TO DO WITH THE SOUL

May God Himself, the God of peace, sanctify you through and through. May your whole Spirit, soul and body be kept blameless at the coming of our Lord Jesus Christ (1 Thessalonians 5:23 NIV).

You are to keep the soul sanctified and blameless. There are two ways you can do this—guarding and renewing your mind.

The first is guarding your mind (see Prov. 4:23). To "guard" means to protect, to shield, or to watch over something and ensure its safety. You need to shield the soul from negative influence, so it is important that you are mindful of the company you keep, the kinds of books and papers you read, and the things you watch on the Internet and television (see 1 Cor. 15:33). You should avoid feeding on unhealthy material. Shut your life against anything that will make a negative impact.

God designed the soul and mind to feed on knowledge or information, and it is always seeking for new information for that reason. In order to realize your full potential in God, you must give yourself to the study of the Word and other godly materials that can build the soul (see Acts 20:32; 1 Tim. 4:13). The more you give yourself to studying the Word, the more the soul is fed, and when the soul is fed, you will gain wisdom, knowledge, and understanding. You can never finish acquiring knowledge. Feed the soul!

The second way to keep the soul sanctified is by renewing your mind (see Rom. 12:1-2). To "renew" means to refurbish, restore, repair, or make good. It means to bring something back to its former glory. The Bible says that we are not of the world, though we are in the world. In the world, we will always encounter the negative—it is all around us. We are always going to see and hear things that are not edifying. In fact, there are things that we cannot avoid catching a glimpse of on the street corner, on the television, or in some seemingly good books. It is the world's strategy of gaining control of our minds and lifestyles. In fact, most of the things we see or hear are negative. Most of the things in the media today are about money, fame, sex, or gossip and other maladies.

We know that what we hear or see gets into our soul/mind and is stored there, and it is what is stored in our souls that influences our behavior. We therefore need to learn to get rid of all the negative influences, because they affect our morality and the quality of our spiritual life. We can renew our mind by meditating on the Word. Through meditation we are able to replace what is in our mental and emotional storage with the Word. By using the Word, we can flush out of our system what is contrary to the will of God.

It is hard for many people to stay quiet in the Presence of God for a prolonged period of time and meditate on His Word and His goodness. This is a deeper level of fellowship and relationship with God. It is another level of spirituality, and the Bible has a lot to say about the need for the believer to give himself to meditation. Through meditation we are able to renew our minds, plant the Word, break the stronghold of the devil, and connect with the spirit realm.

THE SPIRIT

The spirit is the life-giving part of man (see James 2:26). It is the connecting link between God and man (see Job 32:8; Rom. 8:16). When the spirit is weak, it affects the other parts of man, and when it leaves the body, the body dies (see James 2:26). God's original purpose is that the spirit should lead man, not the soul nor the body. God speaks to man through his spirit. Only the spirit of man can hear God, but it is the soul that interprets what God is saying and communicates it to the body. If the soul is not renewed, it cannot rightly interpret what God is saying (see Rom. 12:2; Gal. 5:16,25).

The spirit is what connects us to the Spirit of God. When you are not in tune with God, you walk in the flesh. The spirit ministers supernaturally; it takes from the realm of the divine and it shows it to us. The way of the spirit may go against the voice of reason and feeling. The body and the senses may not feel like it, but it does not matter because in the spirit you are walking in the divine, the supernatural, and the extraordinary. When you walk that way, you start to see yourself the way God sees you—you start to show forth your sonship and manifest the power of God. God is seeking to demonstrate His power, His majesty, and His wisdom through you. Even the creatures cannot wait for your manifestation. When you are walking in the Spirit, you are able to bring the flesh and all its desires to subjection.

This I say then, Walk in the Spirit, and ye shall not fulfill the lust of the flesh (Galatians 5:16).

Only the spirit of man can hear God, but it is the soul via the mind that interprets what God is saying and communicates it to the body. If the mind is not renewed, it cannot rightly interpret what God is saying via the spirit.

And be not conformed to this world: but be ye transformed by the renewing of your mind, that ye may prove what is that good, and acceptable, and perfect, will of God (Romans 12:2).

So to be able to rightly divide the Word or interpret God's will, one must renew his mind. Renewing the mind is all about training the mind to understand the language of the Spirit, which is the Word, viewing the world through the eye of the Word, and interpreting everything within the context of the Word.

Chapter Ten

Achieving Destiny

The fact is that we all are people of destiny. "Destiny" means that before you were born, God had determined what you would look like, who your parents would be, how you would be born, where and into what nationality you'd be born, and what He wanted your future to be like. He said to Jeremiah the prophet:

Then the word of the Lord came unto me, saying, Before I formed thee in the belly I knew thee; and before thou camest forth out of the womb I sanctified thee, and I ordained thee a prophet unto the nations (Jeremiah 1:4-5).

You see, it does not matter how you were conceived. Maybe your mother was raped and she became pregnant with you, maybe your parents never married, or maybe you were a product of extra-marital affairs—it still does not matter, because before you were conceived God had ordained you and had planned a great future for you. Destiny is about what God has in His mind concerning your future. God has a blueprint regarding the final outcome of your life here on earth. God never begins something before knowing what He is going to do with it. Before He begins something, He first defines what He wants it to be. Before you were born, God had finished every work about you.

According as He hath chosen us in Him before the foundation of the world, that we should be holy and without blame before Him in love: having predestinated us unto the adoption of children by Jesus Christ to Himself, according to the good pleasure of His will (Ephesians 1:4-5).

Now, it is important to understand that there are two dimensions to your destiny. The first is exclusively out of your control, and this includes your conception, your family, your color, and your nationality. The second is determined by you. You can determine whether you follow God's plan for your life or not, what future you want to have, who your friends will be, who you will marry, what career you will have, and where you want to live. The fulfillment of what God has in mind concerning your future is largely dependent on you. You did not have any say about your birth, but you have got everything to do with the final outcome of your life here on earth.

There are three things that are important in achieving destiny— understanding God's plan for your life, knowing your destiny-helpers, and following the leading of the Holy Spirit.

UNDERSTAND GOD'S PLAN FOR YOUR LIFE

The first thing you need in order to achieve your destiny is the understanding of what God has planned for your life. If you do not know it, you may spend all your life trying to be somebody else and not who God has created you to be. Some of us admire other people— we admire their color, their chosen profession, et cetera, and we put a lot of effort into being like them. But you need to realize that you are unique, blessed, and created to be just you. It is in knowing the real you and pursuing it that you can find satisfaction and completeness.

Everybody can be happy and very successful in life because we are all born to succeed. Nobody is born to be a loser or a failure.

It is easy to be successful if only we can know the purpose for which we were created and key in to it. When you figure out what you are meant to be in life, make it your vision, your goal, and your passion. Part of what contributes to who we are today are our desires, our visions, and the goals we set for ourselves yesterday. You are today what you saw and worked for yesterday. What happened yesterday is not the real you. Who you are today is not the real you. The real you is in the future. Today is not your limit and it does not matter what you are going through right now—there is something about you that will materialize tomorrow whether the devil likes it or not. But you must find out what your tomorrow is all about and go for it no matter what; then the devil cannot stop you.

What you can see is what you can become. What can you see? A man of vision never dwells on his past—to him that is history. A man with a purpose in life is never satisfied with the present—to him the present is only a passage. A man of vision never gives up hope, and he is not discouraged by now. His strength comes from his ability to see what is ahead of him. A man of vision is never moved by the opinions of others—to him they are only words of men and are irrelevant. His inspiration is the Word of God.

That you have a vision does not mean that you are not going to have challenges. You may experience delay and opposition; you may get fired at work or fail in some important exams. When the going becomes tough, satan will want to make you stop believing in your destiny and going after it. But if you can keep the vision in focus, you will get there (see Heb. 12:1-2).

KNOW YOUR DESTINY-HELPERS

The second important thing in achieving destiny is to identify the people who are assigned to you by God as helpers of destiny. Every one of us has people ordained of God to be his or her helpers. There are things that you may never discover until somebody shows them to you, things that you may never have until somebody gives them to you, and places that you may never go to until somebody comes into your life. Some things do not drop from Heaven because God has put them here on earth. God uses human beings as vehicles of blessing.

There are people who are assigned to you by God and are endowed with something you need that will help you reach your destiny. God will bring such people into your life; it is part of the plan, but it is up to you to identify such people and keep them.

To keep people in your life, you must learn to value people and treat them with respect. If you do not know how to keep people, you cannot get to some levels in life. The devil will want to separate you from your helpers. He will want you to think you do not need anybody. But I tell you the truth—there are things that you will not be able to achieve alone. With the right people in your life, you can in one year achieve what will take others ten years simply because you have helpers. I have seen people push away their helpers and walk out on them. These people always find life tougher than it ought to be.

There are people who have gone ahead of you on this path; they have experienced and conquered the things you are struggling with right now. There are people out there who are blessed, empowered, and assigned by God to inspire you, encourage you, and help you through things in life. It is your duty to find them. These are men and women who have been tested and proven—men and women who have been through summer and winter and still stood with God. God will bring them your way. When you find them, stick with them, make them partners, and be ready to learn from them.

You also need to be aware of destiny-killers. These are people who do not give regard to what you believe and do not care about what you have set out to achieve for yourself. These are people who always want to wear you out, make you sorrowful, make you sin, and discourage you. These are people who make you feel inferior and make your situation look impossible any time you are with them. You need to keep such people out of your life. If you stick with them, they will eventually kill your fire.

He that walketh with wise men shall be wise: but a companion of fools shall be destroyed (Proverbs 13:20).

My advice is to keep away from anybody who is always confessing negative things about what you are doing, who despises what God is making out of you, and who always has dozens of reasons why you will not succeed.

FOLLOW THE HOLY SPIRIT

The third important thing for achieving destiny is knowing and following the leading of the Holy Spirit. You operate under divine wisdom when you walk with the Holy Spirit. You see, there are two kinds of wisdom—worldly wisdom and spiritual wisdom. Worldly wisdom is the right and skillful application of worldly knowledge. You will be walking in worldly wisdom if your action is simply based on the knowledge you have acquired through studies, dealings with people, or your experience in life.

Worldly knowledge can fail you because it is limited. We do not always know all things; only God knows all things. Spiritual wisdom, which is also called the wisdom of God, is the correct application of knowledge received from God. God puts the Holy Spirit within us when we become children of God so that we may know the mind of God (see 1 Cor. 2:9-12). We walk in the wisdom of God, or divine wisdom, when we follow the leading of the Holy Spirit. You can never fail if you are operating in divine wisdom, because it is the way of the Spirit and the Spirit of God can never fail.

> *Thus saith the Lord, thy Redeemer, the Holy One of Israel; I am the Lord thy God which teacheth thee to profit, which leadeth thee by the way that thou shouldest go* (Isaiah 48:17).

WHY FOLLOW THE HOLY SPIRIT?

1. We have limited knowledge and do not know the full plan of God.

There are things about us and about the people we are involved with that we do not know. We do not know what we are going to go through in the future. Only God knows everything, including the future. He lives in the past, present, and the future, and He wants to lead us in the way we should go—the way which ultimately will be for our good.

> *Trust in the Lord with all thine heart; and lean not unto thine own understanding. In all thy ways acknowledge Him, and He shall direct thy paths* (Proverbs 3:5-6).

We are going to get it wrong if we depend solely on our ability or knowledge. The Bible says, "There is a way which seemeth right unto a man, but the end thereof are the ways of death" (Prov. 14:12). To walk with God, you must accept that you are not knowledgeable enough and don't have all the answers. You don't know absolutely everything. What you think is right might damage you. We all need God to show us what to do to achieve great destiny.

2. When we follow God's leading, we will not fail.

A believer cannot fail in following the Holy Spirit because God will not lead us to where we are not going to make it. He will lead us to where we will succeed for His Kingdom. You can only fail when you ignore or set aside His leading over your life. You will experience blessing wherever He leads you. He will never lead you to where you will suffer defeat.

3. Following the Holy Spirit anoints the believer to overcome in spiritual warfare.

Satan regards us as his enemies because of our relationship with God. He hates us because God cares about us, and he hates and wants to destroy anything that God is interested in because he is jealous of God. He once tried to overthrow God, and he still seeks to overthrow the control of God wherever he sees it, including the control of God over our lives. Satan would like to destroy your destiny because it is God's idea. To be victorious over satan, we must follow the leading of the Holy Spirit. We can only enjoy victory over satan when we learn to listen to and follow the leading of the Holy Spirit.

KNOW THE LEADING OF THE HOLY SPIRIT

To know the leading of the Holy Spirit, we must be established in the fact that God has good intentions for us and will not lead us to fail or suffer defeat (see Jer. 29:11). Some believers are afraid to know God's will for their lives, because they think that God might lead them to do something they will not like. They do not want to know what His will is when they have a fantastic job offer or when they have just fallen in love with somebody they would really love to be married to. They are afraid to know the mind of God, because they think God will say something that will destroy the good things that are happening in their life. They do not know God as a good Father, and they are ignorant of the fact that He has their best interest at heart and will never do anything that will not be to their benefit. That is the lie the devil would like you to believe in, but God cares so much about us and has our best interest at heart and will only give us the very best and nothing less.

> *Or what man is there of you, whom if his son ask bread, will he give him a stone? Or if he ask a fish, will he give him a serpent? If ye then, being evil, know how to give good gifts unto your children, how much more shall your Father which is in Heaven give good things to them that ask Him?* (Matthew 7:9-11)

It is also important to understand that we cannot know what the will of God is by simply looking at the circumstances that we find ourselves in. The fact that something appears beautiful does not mean that it is of God, and if the situation is rough and difficult, it does not mean that you are outside the will of God.

> *For the Kingdom of God is not meat and drink; but righteousness, and peace, and joy in the Holy Ghost* (Romans 14:17).

Circumstances can sometimes be rough and still be of God, or they can be rosy and cozy and still be of satan. Sometimes things get really rough and difficult, even in the leading of God. So because things are not going as you expected does not mean that you have missed it. Jesus told the disciples to cross to the other side of the lake, and as they sailed in obedience to His word, the storm still rose against them (see Mark 4:35-39). Remember, they started the journey because

Jesus told them to, and yet they were challenged by the storm and the wind. The experience of the wind and the storm does not necessarily mean that God is not leading you there.

In your walk with God, you will sometimes go through fire or walk through the valley of the shadow of death (see Isa. 43:2; Ps. 23:1-4). Sometimes, God will allow a storm to blow on something you are building even when it is based on His words (Matt. 7:25). This does not mean that you are not in God's will. You may wonder why God would allow such things to happen to someone who is walking in His will. Well, all we know is that whatever God allows or does is always for a good reason. I know God sometimes allows us to go through rough situations so that we can become experienced in life and develop character and mature. I know that God also uses tough situations to make us who He wants us to be. They serve as gateways to our success and destiny.

> *And we know that all things work together for good to them that love God, to them who are the called according to His purpose* (Romans 8:28).

Some challenges have to happen to us for our destiny to manifest; it is part of the plan. To determine whether you are being led of God or not, you may need to ask yourself the following questions.

1. Is what I intend to do or be part of in line with the Word of God?

> *All Scripture is given by inspiration of God, and is profitable for doctrine, for reproof, for correction, for instruction in righteousness: that the man of God may be perfect, thoroughly furnished unto all good works* (2 Timothy 3:16-17).

God is bound to His Word and will never lead you to do something that contradicts His Word. For instance, God cannot lead you to marry somebody who is not born again, because He has said in His Word to not be unequally yoked with unbelievers (see 2 Cor. 6:14).

2. Will what I am about to do or be part of glorify God?

> *He shall glorify Me: for He shall receive of Mine, and shall shew it unto you* (John 16:14).

God will never lead you to do anything that He will not take the glory for. If He will not take the glory for a thing, He will not be part of it because He will not share His glory with any man (see Isa. 42:8).

3. Will it minister comfort, exhortation, and edification to the people it may affect?

Let us therefore follow after the things which make for peace, and things wherewith one may edify another (Romans 14:19).

It will not be of the Spirit to do something that will damage or destroy somebody. He said in His Word that love does not harm others, and God is love (see Rom. 13:10).

4. How do I feel about it on my inside? Do I feel peaceful or condemned? Does it give me joy? How will it affect my standing with God (see Rom. 14:17)?

There are two kinds of peace that the believer enjoys—peace with God and the peace of God (see Rom. 5:1; Phil. 4:7). Through faith in Jesus we now are at peace with God and there is no more enmity between us. Because of Jesus, God will never again close the door against you or treat you like a sinner. The Bible says the Lord is angry with the wicked every day (see Ps. 7:11). But you are now accepted—that is peace with God.

Peace with God is different from the peace of God. We enjoy the peace of God when we are in tune with God, obeying His Word, and walking in His will. We lose our peace when we step out of His will. The loss of peace is an indicator that something has gone wrong in one's walk with God. One of the ways the Lord chastises the believer is by withdrawing the peace of God—this is also called conviction. God convicts so that we will know that something is not right and we can fix it. That was what David experienced when he cut the skirt of Saul's robe (see 1 Sam. 24:5).

Faith is crucial in walking with the Holy Spirit. You have to be able to act by faith to do what you believe He is saying to do. Faith is crucial because the Holy Spirit's instructions will sometimes appear crazy.

The way of the Spirit is not something your flesh will easily accept. So to walk by faith, you must be able to bring the flesh under subjection to the Word.

THE WAYS OF THE FLESH

The flesh communicates in three basic ways, but they are *not* how God wants you to operate.

The Voice of Reason

While the Lord speaks through the Word and the Spirit, the flesh speaks through reasoning. It is not possible to understand God through the use of the senses. God's ways do not make sense to me at all. Some things require the use of your head—crossing the highway, not riding a bike on a motorway, not using a lighter in a gas station et cetera—but it is not so in your walk with God. A lot of times, what He says to do are things that your mind cannot reason out, and it will seem like foolishness to your sensual judgment.

> But the natural man receiveth not the things of the Spirit of God: for they are foolishness unto him: neither can he know them, because they are spiritually discerned (1 Corinthians 2:14).

In 1996, my wife and I attended the inauguration of one of the Redeemed Christian Church of God's (RCCG's) newly formed provinces. At the service, God spoke to us and told us to give the province half of our income for some months. My wife was pregnant with our first daughter at that time, and we were believing God for loads of things for the baby. We did not really have much of an income. God putting us in that position did not make sense to me initially. Giving half of our income for months was terrifying, but we did what He said. It was hard and painful, but we did it all the same. Three months after our baby was born, we received a letter from the RCCG headquarters missions board inviting us to go on a missions trip to Germany. It was then that the Lord showed me that He led us to sow that seed to prepare us for ministry abroad.

Faith is not about using common sense. God is far more than your mind can grasp. What God says may not be sensible to you. It may sound silly, so do not try to rationalize it. All you need to do is to simply obey God, and you will see God respond to your obedience. If you want to walk with God, you will have to make up your mind not to follow your head but to follow your spirit.

The world today finds it difficult to accept the testimony of God, because as far as the world is concerned, it does not tally with good reasoning. It did not make any sense to lay down half of my income for a few months when my wife and I were expecting a baby, but because we acted on faith and obeyed the leading of the Holy Spirit, He opened the nations to us. Today, we are in a place where we can never lack again.

The Voice of Feeling

God does not communicate through feeling. Feeling is the voice of the flesh. Never base your actions on how you feel—you cannot be victorious that way. Faith has nothing to with good reasoning or how you feel. Feeling will mislead you; it misled Isaac when he blessed Jacob in the place of Esau. He could tell from the voice who he was talking with—it was the voice of Jacob, not Esau. But he chose to act on feeling instead, and he blessed the man he did not intend to.

> *And Isaac said unto Jacob, Come near, I pray thee, that I may feel thee, my son, whether thou be my very son Esau or not. And Jacob went near unto Isaac his father; and he felt him, and said, The voice is Jacob's voice, but the hands are the hands of Esau. And he discerned him not, because his hands were hairy, as his brother Esau's hands: so he blessed him. And he said, Art thou my very son Esau? And he said, I am. And he said, Bring it near to me, and I will eat of my son's venison, that my soul may bless thee. And he brought it near to him, and he did eat: and he brought him wine and he drank. And his father Isaac said unto him, Come near now, and kiss me, my son. And he came near, and kissed him: and he smelled the smell of his raiment, and blessed him, and said, See, the*

smell of my son is as the smell of a field which the Lord hath blessed. ...And it came to pass, as soon as Isaac had made an end of blessing Jacob, and Jacob was yet scarce gone out from the presence of Isaac his father, that Esau his brother came in from his hunting. And he also had made savory meat, and brought it unto his father, and said unto his father, Let my father arise, and eat of his son's venison, that thy soul may bless me. And Isaac his father said unto him, Who art thou? And he said, I am thy son, thy firstborn Esau. And Isaac trembled very exceedingly, and said, Who? Where is he that hath taken venison, and brought it me, and I have eaten of all before thou camest, and have blessed him? yea, and he shall be blessed (Genesis 27:21-27,30-33).

Feeling is only going to mislead you if you follow it. If you feel a particular way, that does not mean that God is leading you that way and vice versa. I hear people say, "You do not have to do it if you do not feel happy about it," but in the ways of the Spirit, feeling happy has nothing to do with it. I believe Abraham was not in any way happy when he laid Isaac on the altar and pulled out his sword to slay him. No, he did not feel like it—he was simply obeying God.

The Voice of Sight

God sees beyond now; He sees beyond what is material. He looks into the future. He is destiny-oriented, not now-oriented. The flesh is limited to the present, but faith acts on what God says and not on what the situation says. If you are going to look at what you are seeing, you cannot walk with the Spirit.

For our light affliction, which is but for a moment, worketh for us a far more exceeding and eternal weight of glory; while we look not at the things which are seen, but at the things which are not seen: for the things which are seen are temporal; but the things which are not seen are eternal (2 Corinthians 4:17-18).

To operate in faith, you must learn to see yourself in the light of God's Word, not in the light of what you can see now. Do not allow what the devil is showing you to drown out what you are hearing from God. The devil is a liar. See people in the light of what God is saying. See your marriage, finances, career, and situations in the light of the Word. Do not limit yourself to the physical.

Everything physical comes and goes, because life is a passage. But God has finished a work in you. You are a child of destiny, complete in Christ, and by His Spirit God loves to take you into the destiny He has planned for you. If you will not let the devil force you to dwell on the physical, you will be unstoppable. The devil is a liar. The truth is that you are who God says you are. All you need to do is listen to His Spirit. Do not be misled by the voices of the flesh. If you will be led by the Holy Spirit, you cannot be stopped, you are dwelling in safety, and your future is secured. Your destiny is within your reach.

About the Author

Pastor Musa Bako is the senior pastor of Victory Assembly, a dynamic, growing, multicultural church in the city of Sheffield, UK. He has served in full-time ministry for about twenty years and has been a pastor for seventeen years. He is a motivational conference speaker and teaches the Word of God with clarity and practical insight. His mandate is to resource men and women with tools to succeed in life and fulfill the reason for which they were created. Pastor Musa is married to Pastor Eunice Bako and together they are blessed with three children.

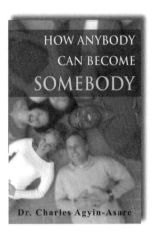

A new exciting title from Destiny Image™ Europe

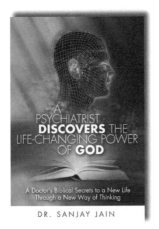

A PSYCHIATRIST DISCOVERS THE LIFE-CHANGING POWER OF GOD

A Doctor's Biblical Secrets to a New Life
Through a New Way of Thinking

by Dr. Sanjay Jain

A Psychiatrist Discovers the Life-Changing Power of God presents the importance of capturing your thought-life and controlling your mind—a profound battle zone. The author combines psychiatric and biblical perspectives about mental, physical, and emotional issues and provides practical steps and strategies about how to overcome a negative mind-set. Break out of the bondages locked in your mind today! This book equips, empowers, transforms, restores, and inspires you to experience freedom and peace in every storm.

ISBN: 978-88-96727-03-4

Order now from Destiny Image Europe
Telephone: +39 085 4716623 - Fax: +39 085 9431270
E-mail: orders@eurodestinyimage.com
Internet: www.eurodestinyimage.com

Additional copies of this book and other book
titles from DESTINY IMAGE™ EUROPE
are available at your local bookstore.

We are adding new titles every month!

To view our complete catalog online, visit us at:
www.eurodestinyimage.com

Send a request for a catalog to:

Via Acquacorrente, 6
65123 - Pescara - ITALY
Tel: +39 085 4716623 - Fax: +39 085 9431270
"Changing the world, one book at a time."

Are you an author?

Do you have a "today" God-given message?

CONTACT US

We will be happy to review your manuscript
for the possibility of publication:

publisher@eurodestinyimage.com
http://www.eurodestinyimage.com/pages/AuthorsAppForm.htm